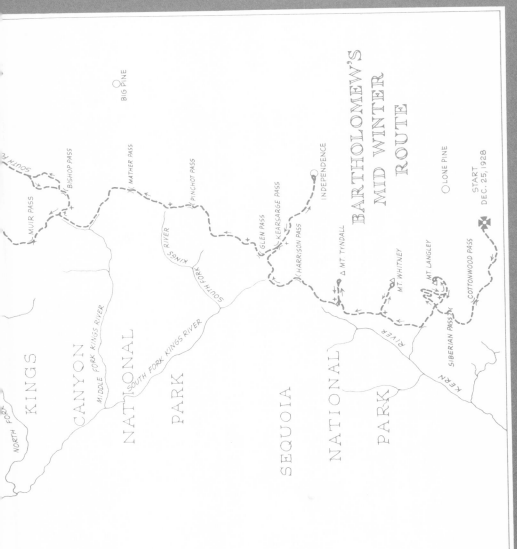

Howard Crawford

KINGS

CANYON

NATIONAL

PARK

NORTH FORK

MIDDLE FORK KINGS RIVER

SOUTH FORK KINGS RIVER

SOUTH FORK

KINGS RIVER

MUIR PASS

BISHOP PASS

SOUTH FORK

MATHER PASS

PINCHOT PASS

BIG PINE

GLEN PASS

KEARSARGE PASS

HARRISON PASS

INDEPENDENCE

△ MT TYNDALL

SEQUOIA

NATIONAL

PARK

KERN RIVER

MT WHITNEY

△ MT LANGLEY

SIBERIAN PASS

COTTONWOOD PASS

LONE PINE

BARTHOLOMEW'S
MID WINTER
ROUTE

START
DEC. 25, 1928

Dave —
I hope you enjoy
the book.
Phil Bartholomew
Dec 8 2004

Best regards,
Gene Rose

High Odyssey

Orland Bartholomew's solitary ski trek—300 miles up the backbone of the Sierra Nevada in the middle of winter—was an heroic feat. Here he traverses a frozen, snow-covered lake on the approach to Mather Pass in the upper reaches of the Kings River.

High Odyssey

The first solo winter assault of Mount Whitney
and the Muir Trail area, from the diary of
Orland Bartholomew and photographs
taken by him.

by
Gene Rose

Panorama
West Books
Fresno,   California

HIGH ODYSSEY

Revised edition

Library of Congress Catalog Card No. 74-83757
ISBN 0-9441-9408-7

Printed and bound in the United States of America

Published by Panorama West Publishing
Fresno, California

Contents

Having achieved the summit of Mt. Langley, Bartholomew photographed
the basin, dominated by The Miter (at left), through which he had made his
first, unsuccessful approach to Mt. Whitney. Almost all the pictures in this
book are Bart's own work.

Introduction

This is the story of Orland Bartholomew and his unbelievable winter exploration of the Sierra Nevada of California, perhaps the most ambitious and adventurous feat by one man during this century. Bartholomew's bold trip of 1928-29, called the Mt. Whitney to Yosemite Mid-Winter Expedition, has remained virtually unknown, aside from a few newspaper stories, for it was not designed to make headlines. While several recent books on the Sierra Nevada have mentioned his audacious journey, the real story has heretofore been untold.

To understand the magnitude of his mission, it is necessary to know something of "his mountains," the Sierra Nevada. This rugged range is the dominant physical feature of California, a formidable, natural barrier along the eastern boundary of the state. One section, the High Sierra, rises above the rest and forms a network of peaks and spires interspersed with deep canyons, rushing rivers and alpine lakes. With altitudes over 14,000 feet, it is a high and often hostile country of many moods and masks.

Over the ages the entire range has controlled entry to the lands beyond. The early Plains Indians led the way: through trial and error they selected the most accessible canyons and passes, and concluded which trails were passable. Those who followed blundered into the great barrier with varying degrees of luck, and many met their match in these mountains. The ill-fated Donner Party became the most infamous, but even today the Sierra still takes a frightening toll from the ranks of the unsuspecting or ignorant.

On Memorial Day 1971, four young climbers perished on the 13,000-foot slopes of Mt. Ritter in the Minarets. Caught by a late-season snowstorm, the climbers froze to death in the bitter cold of a night-long bivouac; one lone survivor stumbled down the mountainside to recount an ordeal of desperation during the lonely night atop the mountain. In 1973, three backpackers died of exposure in two separate areas of the Sierra when an early storm caught them unprepared. During the same year in Yosemite National Park's back country there were eighteen fatalities. Unfortunately, such incidents occur all too often when the unwary test their lives against the might of these mountains.

Today, search and rescue units from the National Park Service or the affected counties perform hundreds of searches each year. Yet despite their presences, the toll continues as more and more winter travelers seek to discover the mystery and the magic that lured Bartholomew to the High Sierra years ago.

If the Sierra is a land of tragedy it is also one of triumph. American mountaineering began here over a century ago with the initial, explorative ascents of Clarence King and Richard Cotter. Even before their time, other mountain men such as Jedidiah Smith, John "Snowshoe" Thompson, John Charles Fremont and Joseph Walker had pushed their way through several parts of the range. Undoubtedly the man who made the greatest mark here was John Muir. Figuratively, Muir made the mountains, and his "Range of Light" made Muir famous beyond his wildest expectations. His eloquent prose and profound geological reasoning established the Scottish immigrant as a giant in natural science, evolutionary philosophies and literature.

While of different backgrounds and diverse goals, these early mountain men shared one thing: a respect for the range and its dangers. With few exceptions they limited their efforts to the short months of relatively good weather. While most felt the sting of the Sierra winter at some time, they were content to exit the high country with the first snows since it was just good common sense not to get mixed up with the "other season." This early vanguard knew what winter meant: its siege can come early and stay late, and its bite means more deep snow, ice, winds, cold, and unforeseen hazards. The elements create huge natural barriers to heighten the feelings of isolation in a white prison from which escape or rescue are equally difficult.

By today's standards, wintering in the Sierra before World War II was infinitely more severe. There were fewer roads across the great barrier, and none was plowed until 1934. For five or nearly six months of the year, the high country was snowbound, with no search and rescue units, no saving helicopters. In 1928 there was only the winter with its cold and snow as it had been for thousands of years.

And yet there was one man ready to test these mountains, Orland "Bart" Bartholomew (1899-1957). Here was the mountain man of all seasons, a winter version of John Muir and then some, for under the most difficult conditions, against the advice of friends and family, Bartholomew alone and unaided undertook the longest, most daring trek in the history of American mountaineering.

By all accounts Bart was a superb mountain man. While many of the old-timers of his generation have passed from the scene, those who knew him praise his many attributes. Some say he was a mountain greyhound and could cover the rough distances of the high country faster than a horse. Others point to his strong will and recall that once his mind was made up nothing could change him. Still others remember his dedication to the mountains. And though he was slight in stature, his zest and quest for life led him to undertake the seemingly impossible.

Though lacking advanced degrees, Bartholomew ranked as a Sierra scholar. During his lifetime, he acquired a mountain of knowledge on both the human and natural history of the great range. For many years Bartholomew served as a lecturer at the summer campus of Fresno State College at Huntington Lake, where his wisdom and knowledge was sought out by students and visitors alike.

The times in which he lived afford further insight into his personality. Bartholomew hailed from an age of heroes—a period when men were really men and adversity was part of life. Although things are easier now, the sterling qualities exemplified in this individual remain ageless and could well be the recipe for recovery from today's disillusioned times. He was a man with the spirit of Charles Augustus Lindbergh and the drive of Jim Thorpe, the stamina of George Mallory and the dedication of St. Bartholomew. And yet he was a modest man, minimizing or downgrading his own accomplishment to the point of disbelief. Fortunately his friends and former associates have now stepped forward and offered the information so vital to understand this enigmatic person.

Ultimately, the question arises, what would lead a man to this type of alpine adventure? Why, against the conventions of shelter and safety, would anyone forsake personal comfort and convenience for such mountain masochism? Why indeed?

As an early hydrographer, Bart realized the importance of winter to the Golden State. Without the white gold of Sierra snows, California would be nothing but a desert. So, to the advancement of this interest, he set about in the 1920s researching and documenting the information, both privately and vocationally. There are, of course, other motivating factors. Mountains have long called spirited men to their bosom and to their battlements. More than being lands of tragedy or triumph, they are lands of tribute and trial. Probably Bartholomew never read Foss' great line, "Bring me men to match my mountains," but match them he did and in a way the like of which we may never see again.

When he crossed that final summit, the family of man lost a magnificent member. It is my wish that this book convey, at least in part, the greatness of Orland Bartholomew. To the preservation of this legacy the present book is dedicated.

The motivations behind this writing are many, as are the acknowledgments of valuable assistance from many fine people. First, Bill Berry, historian for the United States Ski Association and the director of the Western Museum of Skisport, asked me to research the history of ski ascents of Mt. Whitney. Other reports at that time credited the accomplishment to an Austrian skier, Otto Steiner, in the early 1930s, but the trail eventually led to the story of a previous ascent by Bartholomew. Perhaps my real impetus came in 1970, when during a visit to a Fresno sports shop I met three young mountaineers who claimed to have made the "first" winter crossing of the Sierra on skis. After I had politely broken their bubble, I felt compelled to set the record straight and began writing what I had already uncovered of Bartholomew's solitary sojourn.

The big break came on December 24, 1971, when Bartholomew's elder son Phil produced a great Christmas gift in the loan of the missing diary and other records of his father's trip.

In addition to Phil's generosity, I am particularly indebted to Mr. Ed Steen, Bart's lifelong friend and early partner, now retired in Fresno. Without his keen recollection of those early activities, this story could not have been told completely. Other insights into Bartholomew came from John Morrison, Roy Cowden and Glenn Burns. Further assistance was given by Larry Adams, Judson Conger and Howard Crawford, all former *Fresno Bee* staff members.

Eugene Rose

Fresno, California
July 1987

One of the many obstacles that Bartholomew would face was winter storms like this squall sweeping over the peaks above Junction Meadow and Bubbs Creek in the Kings Canyon area. Winds and snow often slowed his travel and fought him on the high passes.

1. Departure

Bart pulled his large pack from the back seat of the old sedan and set it to the side of the dusty road. From the pocket of his rough wool shirt he pulled out money and handed seven dollars to the young driver. He spoke a few words of thanks and stepped back as the driver backed the car around some large boulders and headed back down the road to the Owens Valley.

He stood there a moment and watched the sedan disappear from sight. Only a telltale cloud of dust lingered above the canyon, the final reminder that now he was completely alone. It was Christmas day, 1928, and Bart knew that back home in Big Creek his friends and family were enjoying the blessing of the Yule holiday. Nostalgia and loneliness swept over him; the desolation of the empty canyon and the starkness of the desert background below only accentuated the feeling. It was the cold wind blowing intermittently off the high mountains that brought him to the realization that after months of planning this was his day.

Ahead lay over 300 miles of high mountain travel with all of its mistakes and lessons. Up there, high on the crest of the mighty Sierra Nevada was the path for the most ambitious ski trip ever undertaken by one man, and now it must begin. He glanced to the towering peaks above him as they reached for the sky; peak after peak running forward to infinity. It was a strange but irresistible call that had brought him here to this lonely gateway and the great mountains beyond.

Bart swung the seventy-pound pack to his shoulders with the ease of long habit, picked up his skis and poles. After juggling the skis to his shoulder he crossed the patch of snow that had halted the car and went up the road, ski poles in hand. He moved assuredly, looking ahead for some sign of the trailhead. Occasionally he glanced over his right shoulder, mindful of the huge mountain range that rose ever closer on the horizon line.

His immediate concern was the weather. Light southerly winds were aloft and the sky was streaked with gray. Were these the precursors of a prolonged storm? Bart felt that if his trip were to be successful he had to accommodate the vagaries of the weather. He knew well from nearly ten years of trapping and snow surveying that he could weather a severe snowstorm, but he didn't want to fight a storm at the bottom of a canyon. Somehow he felt he would rather face the elements on one of the higher plateaus.

The words of yesterday's phone call to Sequoia Park ranger Richard Way rang in his ears. "You're heading off into the face of a blizzard!" Way had told him. "I wish you good luck — but. . . ." Bart walked on trying to put from his mind that final word.

After nearly two hours of continuous hiking he came to the trailhead marker at the bottom of Cottonwood Canyon. He was somewhat relieved to know that he was starting at the right place. There had been many foulups already and Bart wasn't familiar with this approach to the Sierra high country. He knew he couldn't make many mistakes in the next 14 weeks, because he was going it alone.

Bart's long journey to this point now seemed like an old dream. Only the bitter disappointment of losing the financial backing of the San Joaquin Travel and Tourist Association still ached within him. The group had reneged on its offer to sponsor the proposed expedition with $1,000. This setback had been a crushing blow to Bart and his early partner, Ed Steen, another rugged mountaineer who subsequently withdrew from the proposed trip.

But Orland Bartholomew wasn't easily discouraged, else he would not have been here. He had overcome other disappointments and difficulties; he would now face the impossible. He went up the rocky trail, climbing higher and higher. Soon the last spots of bare soil surrendered to snow, which increased in depth with each upward step.

Near the 8000-foot level the snow became deeper and Bart put on his new skis. It took just a moment to snap the heel latch of his old bindings, remounted on the untried skis. He shuffled them back and forth across the snow, testing the wax. Finding the snow firm he moved out, figuring he would use the wax he had applied several days earlier.

On the skis his progress improved. He moved over to the south side of the canyon where he found the snow deeper and better for skiing. There were detours around obstructions of rocks and brush, and several times he had to remove the skis to cross the brook that still flowed down the canyon; so every few hundred feet he would stop to rest. Eventually he reached the denser timber of the canyon; higher up he had to avoid a large rockslide that had already spilled across the new snows.

He was stopping to rest more often now: the excitement of the day and the thinning mountain air had combined to tax his energy as he struggled upward; but soon he would be climbing again. The Christmas day was fading already, for long, cold shadows were climbing the far walls of the canyon. He was anxious to make camp, and near the upper rim of the canyon, at an elevation of about 9500 feet, Bart spotted the old lumber mill and selected a campsite on a foot of snow.

By the time he had camp established the light had left the mountains. Only out on the Inyo Mountains, far across the

Owens Valley, was there a last trace of sunlight. He prepared a simple and light meal that first evening, though his appetite was great. He felt very tired — it was always that way for him the first day in the high mountains. He sat by the flickering campfire for a short time, drinking a cup of coffee made from melted snow.

This was the beginning.

2. Bart's Trailhead

Orland Bartholomew's path had never been an easy one; as far back as he could remember his trail had been long and difficult. There had been many years of adversity, beginning shortly after his birth at Calistoga, California, on February 22, 1899. Born frail and sickly, he developed a severe asthmatic condition that debilitated him.

The family's life had come down a similar trail. His mother died when he was only three years old. It was a cruel blow for the ailing lad and left his poor father even poorer and with three young children to raise. The times were tough and his father went from job to job, taking whatever work he could find. It seemed to Orland as though they were always moving, every move introducing him to another doctor who would look at the ailing body and shake his head.

Because of his health, schooling was delayed until he was eight years old. When he finally got around to attending school, he did the best he could, but by the time he finished the eighth grade he had completed his formal education. At 16 he left home and struck out on his own. He tried working as a farmhand on ranches in Northern California, but the manual labor needed on a 1915 farm was too much and he returned home, which had now been relocated in Vallejo. With the navy yards working at World War I levels, Bart got on as a warehouse laborer. The job lasted four months until the employer's physical examination revealed his condition. However, the physician was kind enough to suggest that if the young man wanted to live much longer he should get away from the damp, foggy climate of the San Francisco Bay area.

Around this time his father had remarried and the new family took Orland along to its new home, near Sanger, in the San Joaquin Valley. Another move in 1919 took them to Big Creek, in eastern Fresno County, and this small mountain community became Bart's home town.

Big Creek was booming, having become the center of the Southern California Edison Company's giant hydroelectric complex. Spreading out in the mountains behind the canyon hamlet was a network of dams, tunnels and powerhouses. It was a gigantic construction project designed to provide electricity for the mushrooming Los Angeles area, and it afforded work to any able-bodied man, including Bart's father.

Here in the clean, dry mountain air young Bartholomew soon found his health. While the new town had little cultural or educational opportunities, it provided unequaled recreational and recuperative benefits. Fishing, hunting and hiking were at his doorstep. He welcomed the fringe benefits, gradually overcoming the effects of his earlier illnesses, and rose to young manhood. In October of 1920 he went to work as a construction crew clerk and four months later was promoted to a better job, stream gauger.

Stream gauging was a job he liked well. While it demanded much it gave him the opportunity to travel the Sierra back country, measuring the flow of the streams and rivers of the watershed. The work enabled Bart to grow in other ways and still earn a good salary, doing a job he enjoyed, and one he described as "measuring the volume of the fishes' universe."

Bart stayed at it until May 1923, when he got the wanderlust and his father's invitation to leave home. He traveled north to Fairbanks, Alaska. Unfortunately his travels didn't go too well, he nearly starved before finding employment with the Alaska Railroad as a track patrol. The job wasn't much, and after saving enough money, he quit and headed back to Big Creek, the wiser for his travels.

It was a different young man who returned on October 20 to the canyon town below Huntington Lake. He had seen some of the outside world, but more than anything, he had missed his Sierra mountains. The prodigal son was welcomed home, bringing a new direction to his life. He had matured considerably and he looked upon the Big Creek scene through new eyes and with higher goals. In the past months his mind had been opened by the magic of books; now he had become a voracious reader with new drives and desires.

He sought out a job with his old employer, the Southern California Edison Company, and was promised a gauging job if one opened up in the spring. When nothing else worked out he teamed up with an older stepbrother, Merle, in a trapping operation in the mountains above Huntington Lake. Here they found two abandoned cabins about nine miles apart, which they fixed up and stocked with supplies for the approaching winter. In addition they set out an extensive network of traps, larger than two men would normally handle. By using skis, they figured they could cover the great distances involved and obtain more pelts. Bart had learned to ski during his earlier snow and stream gauging duties; the company had a policy forbidding the use of skis but the gaugers quietly preferred them over the issued snowshoes.

Traveling their traplines the brothers found skis most successful. In the first month of their operation they snared 25 marten and were getting rich. A few days after Christmas, they were caught between the two cabins by a snowstorm, and while they were used to snowy weather, this was a major storm.

Galelike winds flayed the two mountaineers, coating them with snow and ice. They were nearly frozen before they managed to reach the lower cabin. That experience did it for Merle; he figured there must be a way to make a living without fighting the elements.

They skied out to Big Creek together, but on January 9, 1924, Bart returned alone with food and two dozen books in his backpack. He continued trapping, pushing his traplines deeper into the back country. He delighted in his isolation, and the snowbound cabin became his winter Walden, sans pond. During the long nights and the stormy days he took companionship with his printed friends; Thoreau, Muir and Emerson were his favorites. Each trip to Big Creek to deliver pelts saw the solitary skier return to the little log cabin with more such friends.

About the first of March, figuring he had caught most of the marten of the Shorthair Plateau, he turned and headed for home. He was rehired as a stream gauger, and was soon back in the high country.

The stream gaugers were a special fraternity of young men doing a difficult job in a rough area. Basically, the job involved regular measurements of the stream flow in the huge watershed. As such it required much arduous cross-country travel to the gauging stations throughout the vast San Joaquin River drainage. It was hard work: a gauger could expect to work from sunup to sundown. If the trail was choked with snow and took longer, that was part of the job. If there were icy rivers to ford, well, those were the breaks.

They were a hardy lot, admired by their peers and respected by their employers. Part of this came from an esprit de corps nourished by the hardships of their calling. Most of them were mountain men — rough and rugged. Some of them were laced with a touch of masochism, at least it seemed so to the Big Creek townsfolk. They had initiation ceremonies, for example,

Whether by wading into the ice-choked waters or flying over in a trolley, stream gaugers measured the volume and velocity of the Sierra runoff. The data they gathered were basic to estimating the hydroelectric potential of California's mountains.

which would have the new tenderfoot gauger swim a snow-choked stream or spend a night in the back country without provisions or protection from the cold.

As a trapper and stream gauger Bart soon gained something of a reputation as a mountain man. Already his familiarity with the Sierra had been recognized by the company, and in time he was named foreman. As such he assumed added duties, but also made extended studies in more remote areas where the snows and streams had never been measured before.

All this time he was learning — becoming sensitive to the ways of the Sierra. Call it experience, woodsmanship, awareness or mountain wisdom, the young man lived in harmony with his hills. Every free moment found him climbing towards the mountains, and each trip brought him added knowledge. More than just surviving in a region many considered hard or hostile, he thrived on it. Particularly he sought to know more about the high country, and to this end he climbed summit after summit. From these vantage points he would map in his mind the outlying topography; a sense of direction, imperative to such off-trail hiking, he acquired readily. Each landmark, every stream became a reference point, and the location of the big domes and tall peaks were filed in his mental bank of information. Maps he committed to memory by hours of careful examination and study.

While familiar with the Sierra geogaphy, Bart knew the animal and plant life even better. After reading all he could find on the flora and fauna, he systematically began his own identification with drawings and photographs. Soon he communicated with scholars and other recognized experts, to ask questions and to make his observations known to them.

In the fall of 1925, Bart quit stream gauging to take a job on a large estate on Huntington Lake, his main duties being those of a winter caretaker. He felt it was a good break for him

In February 1928, a year before the High Odyssey began, Bart traveled alone into the Sierra at winter. This bon voyage photograph shows how unsophisticated his equipment was. An avid and able photographer, Bartholomew made hundreds of photographs of the snowbound Sierra, as of this scene atop Mount Givens, below.

since it would allow him more time for his mountain study and photography. It also permitted him to fill in, on a part-time basis, on the more involved stream gauging jobs. And during the next two winters he made trips into the back country, well beyond the gauging stations in the vicinity of Florence Lake.

During the winter of 1927-28, Bartholomew acquired a a higher education in the practical art of winter survival. During this hard winter, three trips, six to thirteen days in duration, were made east of Florence Lake. It was familiar territory, and his travels ranged as far back as Muir Pass in the Evolution country of the central High Sierra.

On the first trip Bart was accompanied by his close friend and part-time boss, Sam Griggs, chief stream gauger for the South Fork of the San Joaquin River. Together, on January 10, 1928, they headed up the river towards Evolution Valley, to make an official inspection of this high mountain watershed. It was a well-organized journey, having been planned months earlier, when food and other supplies were cached along the proposed route. With relatively light packs and excellent snow conditions they easily penetrated deep into the mountains, probably deeper than anyone had ever gone into the High Sierra during the winter; fortunately the weather was clear, though cold. The pair collected significant data on the snow-fall and watershed storage, and Bart made several photographs of this high, white world. The trip also marked the earliest official use of skis by Southern California Edison stream gaugers.

Lasting almost a week, it was a memorable trip for both men. They were amazed at the animal life they encountered; instead of hibernating, many animals were active on the reborn, white landscape. Bart and Griggs saw marten, chickadees, Sierra hare, conies, porcupines and coyotes. At their Evolution Lake campsite, they heard a chorus of frogs croaking their winter serenade.

Ed Steen, left, and Sam Griggs enjoy a peaceful moment on the front porch
of a stream gaugers' cabin on Mono Creek.

Then, on February 26, Bart skied over Kaiser Pass, above Huntington Lake, and headed for his first solo challenge of the Sierra winter. On his first day he covered over twenty miles of rough, mountainous country, while climbing 2800 feet in elevation. It was an auspicious start for a big, looping trip off the known trails, covering over eighty miles. Swinging south to Post Corrals meadows in the Kings River drainage, he made a base camp on Punchbowl Lake, on the western slope of 12,000-foot LeConte Divide. From there he ranged extensively into Bench Valley and Red Mountain Basin. It was an ambitious trip, plagued with many problems of high mountain travel. In the lower reaches there was insufficient snow for good skiing; higher up the weather was stormy, blowing, cold.

One major storm caught him near the top of 11,200-foot Hell-for-Sure Pass. Engulfed by low-hanging clouds and blowing snow, he could not determine his direction in the white-out conditions. Apparently confused, Bart wandered atop the appropriately named pass for some time, beset by high winds and coated with snow and ice; his very survival was in question. Finally he skied onto an outcropping of rocks protected by a clump of trees, and managed to bivouac there through a long and miserable night.

He overcame other difficulties and learned from the experiences. Toward the end of the trip his packframe broke; his makeshift repair showed him how the frame could be made sturdier without adding to its weight. He found some of his ski waxes ineffective. Rubber gloves were useless in below-freezing temperatures; extra mittens of wool, he decided, would be much better. Garments of "outing flannel" were not at all what the name seemed to imply. A sewing kit, he wrote in his notes, would go along on future trips. He refined his photographic equipment after his troubles with bright snowscapes and half-frozen equipment.

His skiing skills grew and he felt he could handle himself on almost any terrain in the mountains. Weather ranging from unpleasant to vicious had put him and his equipment to the test and he had won. Not only had his techniques been improved; his confidence in himself grew. He was beginning to feel he could enjoy the battle in most storms and survive in even the worst.

Bartholomew returned to Florence Lake on March 2, having been chased over Fleming Pass by another severe storm. He moved on down the mountainside to Camp 62, an Edison construction camp below the lake. Here he rested a couple of days before heading back up the mountainside for another and more extended trip in the Evolution Country.

Again the weather turned stormy. Slowed by blowing and drifting snow, he reached Evolution Lake on March 9. Here he set up a base camp from which he would make more side trips to adjacent basins and mountains. He found his food cache had been opened by martens who had enjoyed Bart's favorite pre-cooked bacon. On that trip, his photographic file shows he roamed over an extended area of the central crest with no particular travel plan. Several times he was chased to his small tent by the wind and weather, but seldom for long. He was in his true element and relished it. Each storm was accompanied by a lesson for the lone mountaineer, and he accepted the opportunity to learn the vital principles of survival.

Protection from the cold was the main course, and it came with many lessons. For campsites Bart knew he had to avoid the most apparent locations in the valleys and canyons where the cold settles in. Instead he would seek a ridge or ledge, preferably sheltered by a clump of small trees. Firewood would come from these trees, usually lodgepole or white bark pine. Once collected, the wood must not be brought near the fire, lest it absorb the melting snow and freeze. The fire would be built upon exposed rocks if possible. If not, Bart would chop away the snow or ice; as a last resort he would build the fire atop green boughs laid in the snow. And a campfire, he found, was not enough to keep him warm unless he spent much of his time gathering fuel and feeding it to the blaze. This precluded the rest he needed after his daytime activity; so he came to rely on more and warmer clothing and substantial, nourishing food — insulating and fueling his personal furnace. Despite the bitter weather, he managed well. There was a knack to almost every part of camp life, even to drying wet socks by hanging them on boughs near the campfire, but not too near.

Several times during that stormy two-week period Bart heard the thunder of distant avalanches. He learned to ignore the sting of the Sierra cold, to fight the fatigue of high altitude, to survive, even to thrive in this now hostile environment.

From this trip Bartholomew prepared an illustrated report on Sierra snow conditions which he sent to F. E. Matthes, the noted geologist in Washington, D.C. The report showed the average snow depth in this basin to be six feet, while a record ten feet had been measured by other gaugers in 1922.

He returned from this longest adventure on March 19 and a group of his friends were assembled at Camp 62 to welcome the solitary skier home. They crowded about the weather-tanned traveler, pumping him with all kinds of questions about his travels. Some who were there doubted the sanity of Bart's winter campouts, but it should be pointed out that these adventures were not madness nor masochism but methodical preparation. While most of his friends and the public considered the idea of winter camping as ridiculous, a few others knew what he was really doing.

In some sublime moment of these initial trips there was genesis. Somewhere . . . somehow from the profound interaction of man and mountain Bartholomew became committed to

Two stream gaugers take snow measurements near Kaiser Ridge in the Sierra. The primitive equipment dates this 1920s photograph of Bart's co-workers.

the idea of a longer and bolder trip. He had met and matched the adversaries; he knew there would be other storms; winds and cold would again battle him; other high passes and steep trails would test him. And there would be new problems and different obstacles, but he would be there.

It was a strange age, a wonderful age. Half a world away the famous British climbing team of George Mallory and Andrew Irvine had excited the world with their fantastic but fatal assault of Mt. Everest. Mt. Logan, the highest peak in Canada, had just been climbed. The golden age of mountaineering was at its zenith. Adventure called men everywhere. Less than a year before, Lindbergh had flown the Atlantic. Other heroes were readying for the world's stage.

3. Caches

Having considered all aspects of an extended Sierra expedition, Bart concluded that its primary objective would be photography. If the results of the trip equaled his expectations, his future would be assured. He was aware of a successful young photographer by the name of Ansel Adams who was working in nearby Yosemite. Possibly, Bart figured, he could develop in a similar direction; he realized he couldn't be a stream gauger indefinitely, because this was a job for vigorous and young men.

Since he had worked closely with the local photographer from Big Creek, Bob Parker, he thought that something might come from his mountain photography. He had already acquired a reputation with a camera: several of his mountain pictures had appeared in Fresno and Los Angeles newspapers. His friends had heard him praise the great photographic coverage of the *National Geographic Magazine,* and he hoped to do something like that.

While photography would be the prime aim, the trip would also provide opportunity for research and study of the Sierra winter. At that time the importance of the Sierra Nevada to the economic life of California was just being realized, but little was known of this dominant physical and geological feature that was to make the state first in agriculture. While the stream gaugers had made their surveys of the snow and runoff waters of these mountains, little other information was available from winter exploration.

Bartholomew reasoned then that, with multiple purposes, the expedition would benefit by adding a second man — a man equally able in the mountain winter and one who could take motion pictures to supplement Bart's still photography. While Bart had discussed the trip with several of his mountain friends, it was a fellow stream gauger and close friend, Ed Steen, whom he asked to be his partner, early in April 1928. Steen, like Bart, was a superb mountaineer in the prime of life, and in several endeavors such as trapping and firearms Steen was the better of the two. Both had years of stream gauging and snow surveying; equally capable on skis, they knew the rigors and adversities of mountain living.

In many respects the two were well suited for their appointed task. Both were young and dedicated mountain men, embodying the better attributes of that band of hardy pioneers who had opened the West a century before. Some said they were the last of the trapper-frontiersmen — descendants of Jim Bridger and Kit Carson, who had broken the backbone of the continent with their feats of exploration and adventure. But if some looked upon the pair as the last of the old guard, others considered them the heroes of the future.

Once this commitment was made things started to happen. It was decided that Bart, as senior partner, would do the overall planning. In addition he would be responsible for all still photography and keep the scientific records, including the meteorological observations. Steen would be the movie photographer, making 16-mm motion pictures of the trip; he would also pass on to Bart his observations of animal life.

Through the effort of several friends, arrangements were made with the San Joaquin Travel and Tourist Association of Fresno to sponsor the expedition. In return for the exclusive publicity rights to the trip, this promotional organization would pay the two $1000 and provide the motion picture camera and film. Once they had a financial backer, planning was begun in earnest and any spare time was spent over maps and supply lists. Heavy correspondence passed through the Big Creek post office as arrangements were made and preparations for all contingencies were discussed.

After considerable thought, the pair decided that the trip should run south to north, an itinerary that would allow them to exit closer to home. More important, it would bring them into Yosemite Valley, which from a publicity standpoint was much better than the uninhabited area around Mt. Whitney. After the direction of travel was selected they had to decide about timing. When, exactly, should they depart and how much time should they allow? At first Bart figured he could cover the 300-mile distance in a month, but on reconsidering the aims of the trip, he added two weeks. When he recalled some of the big storms, he realized that he should add time to weather them, if he and Ed were pinned down. Then he started figuring the elevation they would have to climb and descend in crossing a dozen major mountain passes: it added up to over 70,000 feet, and he added two more weeks to the trip. Next he realized they had to have time to bring film and reports out to civilization, another ten days. The number of days snowballed, increasing with every turn, until Bart concluded they would need the entire winter, and for the trip to be successful, they should head out as soon as there was sufficient snow for good travel.

As for news releases and photography, these too were included in the final planning. Bart arranged that all phases of the photographic processing would be handled through Bob Parker's studio at Big Creek. Parker would develop the films and maintain an indexed file; in addition, he would be compensated for seeing that the sponsoring group received prints for its news releases of the trip.

The biggest problem for such an undertaking would be sustenance, an Herculean job of supply. They decided on a series of caches at intervals along the proposed route; as finally developed, their plans called for 11 caches at distances of about 25 miles. In May they pooled their meager finances to start purchasing for the caches. For each they bought a thirty-gallon garbage can; these they painted a dark green. They would suspend the cans high up in clumps of trees off the trail, out of sight of any mountain hiker or hunter. Sizable quantities of food and other camping supplies were being assembled in the Big Creek store. Each cache was to contain fifty to sixty pounds of food — enough to last the two men for two weeks if necessary. Six of the containers were shipped to persons or places on the eastern side of the Sierra. In addition, a pair of well-used packhorses were purchased to carry the caches up into the mountains.

The caches were designated by location. For example, in the southern region there were the Langley, Whitney, Tyndall and Kearsarge caches, named after nearby mountains or high passes. The first cache they installed was at Devil's Postpile with the assistance of a commercial packer from Mugler Meadow. This northernmost cache was made in July, but it wasn't until mid-August that the young mountaineers left Big Creek, ready to set up the rest of their supply line. Heavily laden with their immediate supplies, they took one cache and headed towards Parcher's Camp on the east slope of the Sierra and about 12 miles west of Bishop. Moving along slowly they passed through Humphreys Basin, over Piute Pass, thankful that they had horses big enough to carry the load. They arrived at Parcher's Camp on August 20 and to their dismay discovered that the cache they had shipped to the resort owner, W. B.

Near this alpine meadow along Rock Creek, Bart and his early partner, Ed Steen, placed the southernmost of the food caches, the one at Langley. Here Ed tends their two packhorses, each loaded down with two of the garbage cans, while Bart takes the picture.

The expedition to set out caches was not all a walk through shady meadows. Ed leads the packhorses Midget and Bird down the rough trail on Junction Pass. In 1928 the trail system along the High Sierra crest was still incomplete; so, even in summer, travel to the 11 cache sites was no easy matter.

Parcher, was undelivered. He volunteered to go down the mountain the next day and try to locate the can and supplies in Bishop. Bart and Steen arranged to spend the night.

That evening as they dined with other guests the conversation naturally included a lot of mountain talk. One of the guests casually mentioned that the dumbest thing he had ever heard of was the trip "a couple of idiots" were planning from Mt. Whitney to Parcher's that very winter. He even inquired if Bart and Ed were doing packing for that trip. Needless to say, little more conversation followed the pair's admission that they were the "idiots."

Parcher returned two days later, having been unable to locate the supplies. Disturbed by the whole affair, the two mountaineers saddled up and headed for the high country around Bishop Pass. For the next week they forgot about the caches and enjoyed the mountains around the Palisades. Fishing, climbing and photography highlighted their mountain wandering. Limits of fish and the summits of high peaks became the goals of each day. They moved along, however, making a big U-shaped trip through the Kings Canyon country, arriving in Cedar Grove on August 27.

Moving up Bubbs Creek the following morning, they climbed nearly 8000 vertical feet to Kearsarge Pass. Near this spot they made an incomplete cache on August 30. From there they dropped over the pass and descended to the little valley town of Independence, where luck was with them, as supplies consigned to A. W. Bidwell were waiting. They packed up immediately, went back to Kearsarge Pass and completed the cache two days later. Though heavily laden they continued down the crest, making a difficult and detoured crossing of Kings-Kern Divide.

Bart and Ed arrived at the southern end of the High Sierra on September 5. Pulling into the Cottonwood Lodge, they found more supplies waiting — two garbage cans and enough food for three caches. They stayed long enough to shoe their pack animals and then headed back up the mountains, crossing Army Pass the following day. This pass was a shorter approach to the forks of Rock Creek, where another cache — designated Langley — was installed. Since neither partner had ever been in this area before, they spent a day around camp. Bart went fishing and Ed scampered to the top of nearby 14,000-foot Mt. Langley.

While it was a period of hard work and travel, it became a memorable summer of idyllic activity. But already fall was in the air; the days had become shorter, touched with the aura of Indian summer. The nights were cooler, and Bart had noted, that night ice was forming on the high lakes and in some of the wetter meadows. The two travelers sensed the change and reluctantly moved on, placing the Whitney caches two days later on the western slope of Mt. Whitney, near Crabtree Meadow.

From there they moved up the Kern River Canyon towards Shepherd Pass, and on September 10 Bart placed the Tyndall cache nearby. In both instances Ed took time to hike to the summit of two more 14,000-foot peaks while Bart busied himself with the last-minute details of the cache, describing their contents in his diary.

For the rest of September, they worked their way northward, installing caches as they went. The combination of heavy loads and poor trails gradually caught up with their packhorses, slowing their progress. Fortunately, the weather held, and after a harrowing crossing of Shepherd Pass, where they were caught in a rockslide, they moved on. After making the Cardinal cache in the upper reaches of the South Fork of the Kings River, one horse became severely lame. Their fair progress slowed to a crawl, and time was running out, as were supplies and money. The two had become concerned about the sponsor's advance money but figured they would find it once they got home. Their immediate problem was to get the Palisade cache installed.

They separated after reaching Little Pete Meadow, Ed and the lame mare heading for Florence Lake, and Bart bound for Parcher's Camp. There he found the missing supplies. He also met the outstanding mountaineer of the Sierra, Norman Clyde, who was already famous for more first ascents of Sierra peaks than anyone. The meeting of the two mountaineers was probably the least heralded union of two of the best men ever to come down the trail. Before the day was over, Clyde had tentatively accepted Bart's invitation to join the winter expedition.

Bart took off the next morning, back over Bishop Pass to an area known as Duzy Basin. where he set the Palisade cache. It contained more food and film than any other cache. Bart felt they would want every opportunity to explore and photograph this area, and a large cache was necessary. Once the cache was placed, he too set off for home. As he came through Evolution Valley, Bart met a party of young mountaineers from Stanford University who were placing caches for a Christmas trip.

Ed had preceded Bart back to Florence Lake by one day. Upon arrival Bart found the lame horse in the corral and a note from Ed explaining that he would be at Sam Griggs' place at Camp 62. When they finally got together they started sorting through six weeks of accumulated correspondence. Despite the many letters, it took but a few seconds to find the one they were looking for. While they had hoped the letter would contain a check, they could have understood if the promised payment had not been included. Instead they were stunned; after they had read it together they passed it back and forth several times to be sure they had read it correctly. They stood there in disbelief and silence for a long time before either spoke.

It was the letter from the San Joaquin Travel and Tourist Association in Fresno. The board of directors of the organization had reconsidered their sponsorship of the trip, and concluded that though the expedition had considerable merit, they were withdrawing financial support. The only explanation was that the group felt publicity of a winterlong snow trip would not be the way to lure travelers to the San Joaquin Valley.

Had it not been for the investment of the past months, the two mountaineers might have accepted the verdict more easily. All the effort in placing the caches had been justified by the belief that it eventually would be compensated. Bart, especially, had already devoted the better part of the year to the trip. All their savings had gone into buying and placing their supply caches.

They didn't even bother to open the rest of the mail. Bart slipped quietly outside and sat down on the stair, looking off to the distant mountains. Ed followed but walked on down the hillside and out of sight.

While Ed had expressed some doubt about continuing the expedition earlier, this was the clincher. He found Bart the following morning and told him the inevitable: he couldn't afford to be unemployed any longer; instead he would spend the coming winter trapping in the area of the Shorthair Plateau. From his experience in this field he figured he could make enough money to tide him over until he could hire on again as a stream gauger. Bart quietly accepted Ed's withdrawal, for he too had great reservations about the situation. Months earlier, when Ed had joined the expedition, they had designed their own expedition flag with the abbreviated "Barsteen" lettered across it. In Bart's mind the pennant now came down the pole. It was a sad and shameful end to an endeavor for which the team had labored so hard.

Bart didn't say much, which wasn't unusual. He busied himself the rest of the day getting six weeks of camping out of his hide, hair and clothing. Inwardly he was trying to justify

Bartholomew and Steen prepare to install the Whitney supply cache to the west of that great mountain seen in the center distance.

a decision he had made months earlier, but in the evening he was back at the pile of mail, quietly reading the letters.

He was going! Come hell or high water his plans were never in question. He was going to Yosemite along the crest from Mt. Whitney, alone. Those who had questioned the whole business from the onset were even more dumbfounded when word filtered back to Big Creek that Bart was still going. The doubters and the skeptics had a field day in the local general store, proposing all kinds of "what-if" disasters. Storms, avalanches, accidents, wild animals and illnesses were just a few of the possible calamities foretold by those who heard of this risky, if not foolish, solitary trek up the crest of the mighty Sierra.

Bart didn't give them much thought. He was too busy reorganizing the trip. Already snow flurries had fallen, and the aspen trees wore their fall colors. Much remained to be done to complete all details of the now one-man trip.

Ed assigned his share of the packhorses, supplies and caches to Bart, knowing that he would still need them. Bart, traveling alone, placed the three remaining caches in the next two weeks. The Humphrey cache was placed below Hutchinson Meadow in French Canyon, about 23 miles east of Florence Lake. On his return he swung back to Evolution Lake, and placed the Evolution cache in the clump of trees at the north end of this very popular alpine lake. About a week later, on October 11, the last cache was set near Silver Pass, in a snowstorm. This cache was installed two miles up Mono Creek to the side of Silver Pass.

Bart returned home assured that he would have ample supplies for the long odyssey. Nearly 800 pounds of food, film and other supplies had been placed in 11 different caches. Originally, the two hikers had planned a food allotment of four pounds per man a day. Since the supplies had been purchased earlier, Bart kept the size of the last three caches as planned, figuring Norman Clyde might still go in Ed's place.

Atop the Sierra, at 13,000 feet near Junction Pass, Ed rests the horses. Steen assisted Bart in placing the supply cans but withdrew from the winter expedition when financial sponsorship failed to materialize.

Phil, Bart's elder son, examines the wide range of nourishing foods that remained in one of his father's supply cans after 44 years. The cache was recovered in October 1972 near Rae Lakes, in the Sequoia and Kings Canyon national parks.

In those caches was the latest then available in canned, condensed and dried food, light in weight yet nourishing. Bart and Ed had written many letters, made many inquiries seeking dried eggs, dried whole milk, and dessicated potatoes, and felt they had a sophisticated menu of varied high-energy foods. Such foods were imperative, Bart decided, since each man's pack with all the necessary winter gear would weigh more than sixty pounds, not including skis and poles.

Bart in his meticulous way had noted every aspect of each cache, preparing a separate map detailing each location. In addition to the map, a photograph was made of the cache so that it could readily be found. Nothing was left to chance. Every item of each cache had been detailed in another notebook.

For example, the location of the Silver cache was described in Bart's notebook:

This cache is about 2 miles up the Muir Trail from the North Fork of Mono Creek. After the first 500' climb from the North Fork, the trail follows up the West side of a small stream, N-NW, for about a mile where it crosses to the East side of the stream and climbs up NE. Follow up the stream about 250 yards and then take up a draw running N-SW, SE-S of a smooth granite bluff. The cache is about 200 yards up this draw in a clump of Hemlock, about 8 feet above the ground, on the upper side, and about 12 up from the lower side. The Hemlock range of 1' to 2.5' in diameter, and are 80-90' high. There are two or three more similar clumps in the same draw.

This self-portrait shows some of Bart's special equipment. The large, heavy pack is topped with his bulky down robe, and protruding above is the helve of a double-bitted ax. The ski poles are hickory—the handles of garden rakes; the six-foot-long skis, made to Bart's specifications, were shorter and wider than the usual sport skis. To obtain this picture, Bart used a special self-timer on his camera, which was a simple Kodak shooting roll-type film. He had no complaints about the photographic equipment, except that the cold froze up "the mechanism"—his word for shutter. So, to protect it, he carried the camera inside his heavy parka.

4. Across the Divide

On December 29, 1928, Bartholomew's commitment to the crest of California was made with the crossing of Cottonwood Pass at the southernmost end of the High Sierra. He was four days from his starting point, 11 miles away and 6000 feet below. Now he had entered a high empty world of thin air and seemingly limitless snow.

The actual crossing of the 11,200-foot mountain pass was relatively easy; there was no signficant aspect to mark the climb. He stopped atop the pass to take a few photographs of the broad rolling scene — a bleak undulating landscape which failed to impress him. Compared to the High Sierra he knew best, this southern part of the range seemed unexciting, soft and gently formed. Only to the north towards Cirque Peak and Mt. Langley did the view resemble the rugged Sierra around his home.

But there were other aspects to this eventful day. He thought of the dozen or so high passes still ahead. None, he was sure, would be as easy as Cottonwood; some would be most hazardous, hostile, and he wondered if they would deny him. He hoped not, but he was committed to finding out. Other thoughts entered and excited his mind: Hannibal's crossing of the Alps, but Hannibal had elephants and surely someone to talk to in the vast army he took across those forbidding mountains. And then Bart felt lonely; at this fateful point any other

Near Cottonwood Pass, Bart photographed these views: above, a snow-dusted unidentified peak; below, Horseshoe Meadows and the rolling high country southeast of Lone Pine.

solitary traveler would have stopped and probably turned back, but not him. He simply appraised the situation, knowing the magnitude of his task and respecting the mountains. After years of exposure to their fickle ways he knew he could not trifle with the Sierra, especially at winter, but there was no thought of retreat.

He shrugged off the feeling of loneliness. Then he shut the imaginary door and pushed his skis down the far side towards Whitney Meadows, three miles away and about 1500 feet lower. As he viewed it from the pass the meadow appeared as a great expanse of whiteness practically surrounded by forest.

And then he was moving downward. He had noticed his new skis felt somewhat strange on the ascent of the pass; going downhill he thought they were tricky, almost difficult to control. The skis meant much to Bart, as considerable time, energy and planning had gone into their creation. A year earlier he had recognized that the sporting variety of skis for that period were too long for cross-country travel; thus he had convinced the Northland Ski Company of St. Paul, Minnesota, to make these special skis nearly two feet shorter but an inch wider. They were the only untested piece of his equipment. He found their six feet of laminated hickory easier to turn, but the added width created all kinds of edging problems. Several times he came close to falling, yet they were all the skis he had and on them he had a long journey to make. He tried to protect the skis, dodging rocks and branches which still protruded through the snow; so he contoured to the meadow by a slower, longer route, avoiding a more direct descent which he thought too steep and obstructed. Although he had applied two types of ski wax earlier, the snow seemed sticky and his progress sluggish.

Just above the meadow he found a small flat and set about making camp. It was a routine he knew well: tent, wood, fire and finally food. As he took the food bag from his pack, he

At Siberian Outpost Meadows the "mountain greyhound" paused to study the bleak winter background of the Sierra. He would be living among those high peaks for the next three months.

realized how his stomach had lightened the load on his back. Five days' sustenance had come from his pack, but he knew he was only ten miles from his first supply cache; so he ate heartily. He cleaned his dishes in the flickering light of the campfire and made ready to turn in. Before crawling into his down robe in the little tent he took a last look at the sky. His check of the heavens — a familiar habit of all mountaineers — gave him reassurance. No storm seemed evident, and while he would welcome more snow for skiing, he was pleased not to see an impending storm this early in his travels.

Bart rose early the next morning and climbed towards the north, to the saddle marking Siberian Pass. It took him most of the morning to reach the top of the ridge, 10,700 feet in elevation. Once there he again shucked his pack and took more pictures.

Departing, he left the snow-covered trail and turned cross-country to the bleak and barren plateau called Siberian Outpost — an area he found to be all its name implies. The wind-swept, treeless expanses seemed desolate, empty except for several large Sierra hares that scampered away as he approached. Bart poled across the vast plateau with a feeling of utter isolation and mystery sweeping over his body. The graying day only heightened the feeling, and once across the void he was ready to make camp above the rim of the bare meadow.

Considering the gloomy nature of the area, he found a suitable campsite in the trees above. There was an outstanding view to the north of the Rock Creek drainage and the fractured skyline of the Sierra crest beyond. There was ample firewood, and by the time camp had been made the weather had improved even though a strong wind blew unceasingly across the vast snowfield just below him. He could imagine what the region would be like in a big storm and he said a silent prayer of thanks for the clearing sky.

Orland Bartholomew's bedroom was this little tent pitched on top of the snow, as here near Evolution Valley. The top is suspended from a yoke of cord tied between two branches, and more boughs have been pressed into the deep, soft snows to provide support. The waterproof floor is the light-colored material showing at bottom right.

Fresh tree boughs were easy to come by and he laid a thick mat of them to pitch his tent on. The snow was hard, wind-packed and about 24 inches deep. Although he had done it many times, Bart always seemed to take pleasure in setting up the complicated little shelter he called a "Cubist's nightmare." The tent's peak required but one suspension point, and Bart soon found a long branch of a nearby tree. Then he unfolded the many parts, pinning down the corners with makeshift tent pegs. It was just six pounds of shelter, including the waterproof floor and ventilating flaps, but it assured him the necessary protection from moisture and wind in the high country.

His dinner, heated in the campfire, was canned corned beef, canned peas and dessicated potatoes reconstituted with snow water; a cup of strong coffee concluded the meal. Then there were the usual camp chores, followed by a few minutes of meditation and the entry into his little diary:

To east end Siberian Outpost Meadows, elev. 11,100.

Ave. snow depth, 2 ft.

This was the shortest daily summary he wrote during that long winter.

5.

Failure at Whitney — the Climb of Langley

Until Alaska was admitted to the Union, Mt. Whitney reigned as the highest mountain in the United States. The Sierra peak is a jumbled mass of crags and spires, pushing its barren summit 14,495 feet into the blue California sky. When viewed from the Owens Valley it seems lost or undistinguished from a dozen neighboring mountains, yet Whitney is the peak that every Golden State mountaineer wants to climb.

Whitney was first conquered in 1873, and since then thousands of climbers have made the summer trek from the Whitney Portal trailhead with relative ease. A winter ascent is a different story, for once the mountain is frosted with snow it becomes a white monster. The trails become choked; the ridges, once warmed by the sun's rays, soon turn to ribbons of ice; and while the actual summit might be free of snow, unbelievable winds, frigid cold and winter's short days make such a climb extremely hazardous.

It will never be known when the idea of a winter ascent first flashed through Bartholomew's mind. From years of mountaineering experience he knew the task would be especially difficult. After a summer climb in 1928, Ed Steen advised him against a winter attempt, but Bart figured it could be done. However, he was well aware that most mountaineers are guilty of making overly ambitious plans in the lowlands and then have to live up to those plans once they are on the high walls.

During the summer of 1928, Bart had corresponded also with the Sierra Club to determine if a winter climb had been recorded. After considerable investigation the club's secretary replied in the negative, but suggested that Bart contact Norman Clyde. The organization felt that if anyone had made a winter ascent it would be that great Sierra climber. Bart subsequently wrote Clyde, who at that time still hadn't decided whether he would join the expedition. Clyde answered promptly, disclaiming any winter ascent of the highest peak; he also declined the earlier invitation, explaining that he wasn't familiar with the use of skis, and the trip was just too ambitious.

With the winter title open, Bartholomew began his battle plans. After examining the topographic maps he realized the necessity of avoiding the precipitous east face of Whitney as too dangerous. He therefore decided on a circuitous approach from the south via Cottonwood Pass with thrusts at the high summit either from the south along Rock Creek or from west of the great peak along Whitney Creek.

Thus on the last day of 1928 the assault was launched. From his bleak camp at Siberian Outpost Meadows, Bart moved out, pushing his skis northward. The weather remained clear and his progress was excellent with two feet of snow covering his pathway. By midmorning he had moved into the Rock Creek drainage. Throughout the day, whenever he paused his gaze would search the skyline for the hidden form of Whitney's summit.

The thought and excitement of Whitney had done strange things for the lonely traveler. For months now the mountain had fired his imagination. Hours and days had been spent over maps, tracing each elevation line that Bart knew would be a barrier or hardship. Many times the problems of such a climb had been magnified in his mind. Big mountains, he knew, have a special way of avoiding capture: there are always obstacles —

A maze of mountains, each a face of vertical chutes, comprises the view towards Mt. Whitney from the south. In this terrain Bart made his first approach to Whitney, which lies on the horizon at upper left. The photograph was taken from the summit of Mt. Langley.

most of them natural — but sometimes the barriers exist only in the climber's mind.

By noontime he had set a camp not far from the Langley food cache, a half mile below timberline on Rock Creek. Once established, he checked the cache then made an explorative thrust at Whitney Pass by skiing up the frozen creekbed to a large basin holding several snow-covered lakes. There he estimated that the summit lay nearly ten miles away and almost 5000 feet above. Moving higher he came upon a series of ice-coated ledges on whose hard surface his skis held poorly. After an hour of struggling to gain a higher ridge, he realized that he could not reach the summit before darkness fell.

He returned to camp and started a fire. It was an excellent campsite with ample dry wood on the nearby trees. While awaiting supper he took a side trip to a ridge in back of camp where he could get a closer look at the approach to the big mountain. His timing couldn't have been better: the sun had slipped low in the winter sky, raking the walls of the mountain amphitheater with the warm colors of alpenglow. So lighted, the ridges and buttresses sprang from the crest, complementing and contrasting with the cold shadows which formed an abstract pattern of mountain magic. Bart's eye ran quickly up the scarred mountainside, searching for a route that might lead him to that elusive summit.

In a moment the magic of alpenglow ended and the glitter that had radiated from the opalescent ice vanished. Almost instantly the relative warmth was erased with the biting cold of high winter. Bart stood there a long time, unaware of the dropping temperature, still facing the mountain and looking for a route that would bring him up to that high point where the stars were now gathering.

He returned to his lonely camp and finished supper, then built up the fire and, by its glinting light, washed dishes. Before long he moved to the confines of his little tent and down bed, but he didn't sleep well that long night. Despite the protection of his camping equipment, sleeping on the snow was never easy, and while the pine boughs afforded some insulation from the cold snow, the mountain was on his mind, precluding the sleep a high traveler needed for a summit try.

Nevertheless he arose early the next morning, well before dawn. It was bitterly cold. He finished breakfast and mounted the skis, squeaking over the light snow that rested atop a frozen pack. By the time the sun finally crept over the great escarpment he had left the cold of the canyon, climbing above Sky Blue Lake. At this point he ran into his first obstacle, a giant barrier of ice-coated ledges looming overhead. His first attempt to surmount them by moving towards the uppermost lakebed came to naught; so he retraced his path and then veered off to the far left side of some unidentified ridge. Here, at the expense of much time and hard work, he gained additional altitude. Repeatedly, the skis skidded dangerously on the rock-hard snow. Every step upwards was forced, the slender edges of the skis being slammed into the snow so they might provide some restraint.

Still he labored upwards. Two thousand feet of difficult climbing finally brought the tenacious mountaineer to the base of a series of chutes. Above this spot the maps indicated a saddle or couloir running off towards Mt. McAdie; if he could gain this elevation, he figured he could then proceed to the final summit over the established upper trail.

The chutes, an intricate maze of broken and serrated gullies, ran upward in many directions, blocking his view beyond. Bart moved precariously to the base of this obstruction. Here the snow and ice were thinner, having been eroded by wind and exposure, and in many spots the warm-colored granite rocks protruded above the glare ice. He started up one of the chutes, sidestepping now, carefully thrusting the sharp points of the ski poles into the frozen surface. A hundred feet up the gully the ascent became more difficult; several times he dislodged snow and ice only to see it tumble far down the steep mountainside and out of sight. Finally Bart was overwhelmed by a sickening conclusion: to continued upwards would only invite disaster, for the pitch of the chute had increased to a point where only ice could cling. If he should slip, the fall would eventually be fatal. So the lone adventurer reluctantly started downwards.

Immediately the threat of disaster became more real for the young man. Several times the skis skidded and nearly lost their slim hold on the mountainside. Disappointment in not reaching the summit was replaced by desperation and the danger of the descent. Now the risks of solitary travel came crashing upon Bart. Any accident — even a simple one — would condemn him to death. A swift, fatal fall, he gloomed, would be preferable to the slow, agonizing finality that would result from a minor accident. Slowly he inched his way downwards; after two hours of tension he reached a slope where normal skiing was possible. But another day had passed and the summit had not even been seen. He raced the lengthening shadows back to camp, contemplating his next approach and thankful that there would be a tomorrow.

Mountains make strange magic for men, but in defeat they take their toll: for Bart that night the price again was sleeplessness. The failure to reach Whitney's mighty summit was a matter he could not force from his mind and so he tossed and turned. Over and over the disappointment denied him the sleep he would need to gain that lofty peak.

But there were other things to trouble him — real things, not the many hardships of living in this hostile environment, nor the loneliness in the empty and inaccessible heartland of the great mountain range. Somewhere in the late part of the distant night, in that twilight area between sleep and consciousness, Bart sensed something unusual. He heard the little tent flapping and the trees swaying to the strange winds that had come up. Their disquieting ways forced him back to reality and Bart inched out of the protective warmth of his down bag. He poked his face out into the inky coldness and immediately noticed the winds had changed direction and were increasing in velocity. Although he could still see the stars, he figured that the predicted and long over-due storm had set a collision course for his special world.

This was warning enough for anyone with a decade of mountaineering; Bart arose and struck camp by daybreak. He moved back down Rock Creek for half a mile to a more timbered and protected site. Here under darkening skies he spent part of the short day constructing a makeshift, Indian-style lean-to called a "wickiup." He had learned this technique, as well as the skills of "siwashing" (camping without shelter) from earlier mountain men, and it took him several hours to cut the boughs and make the snug shelter. Following dinner, he completed the arrangements by pulling the little tent and sleeping gear inside, just about the time it started snowing.

He slept well that night, protected from the storm that swirled above. It was still snowing lightly when he awakened the next morning. With a tape measure he had brought along he measured but four inches of new snow, and his small recording thermometer indicated a minimum of 18°. The wind had changed direction again while increasing; at the campsite its force was moderate but above he could see giant snow banners being ripped off the high peaks. After searching the threatening skies for any hint of clearing, he postponed immediate plans for travel and prepared a big breakfast of hotcakes, canned bacon and coffee. It was a sumptuous morning meal by any

This pine-bough
wickiup protected the
lone mountaineer from
storms he encountered
along Rock Creek in
the first week of 1929.
Through the entrance,
reflected light shines
on tin cans from the
Langley cache.

standards and Bart ate well, knowing the nearby cache held enough food for a month if necessary. With the meal ended, he scoured the pots and pans with chunks of frozen snow and finished by splashing them with steaming water. By late morning with the temperature barely above 20° he concluded the weather wasn't going to improve, so settled down in camp, limiting his activity to the now familiar and regular duties of gathering wood and writing in his diary.

The storm passed that night and the skies cleared with the temperature dropping to a frigid seven above zero. Bart was up early and, once finished with breakfast, he headed for the cache with no other plans for the day.

Still the high mountains were calling. Having food from the cache in his pack, he decided to swing to the southeast and explore the country around Army Pass, several miles south of Mt. Whitney. Travel was relatively good as he skied around the towering flanks of the Major General and Mt. Langley and onto the approaches to the pass. In the new snow his skis were slow despite the frequent waxings, but he considered the waxing a cheap price for the additional cover now atop the rocks and brush. He arrived at a ridge north of the pass by midmorning, finding it nearly free of snow. After a brief picture session he turned his attention to Mt. Langley which loomed above.

And then it happened: soon he was climbing Langley. Up the ridge he went, picking his way through the thinning snow. A natural pathway invited him upwards and before Bart realized it he had climbed above the loose snow, near the 13,000-foot mark. He continued the unplanned ascent with his skis slung over his shoulders; while he had considered leaving them, he realized it might be difficult to find them when descending.

So on he went. Climbing became more difficult, and handholds were often necessary. Other times toeholds were kicked into the hard snow, but when the wind-packed surface was too hard, Bart used the sturdy ski poles, driving in the steel points to brace as a foothold for another step upwards.

As the great landscape receded below the lone climber the air became colder and thinner, requiring frequent rests. On such occasions he would examine the vast winter vista. While the upper slope of the mountain blocked his northward view, everything else lay open to inspection: behind him the mountains dropped sharply to the desert, interrupted only by long ridges and moraines. Here the harsh effects of winter awed Bart, who was amazed to find many peaks bare just one day after a storm. Only the cold and sheltered northern chutes still held snow. The rocky ridges and other exposed slopes had been swept clear by gale winds, and even on the highest peaks snow could be seen only in chutes and chimneys which offered a partial windbreak.

Bart struggled upwards and about 500 feet below the summit swung to the east, where he could look down upon the mantled Cottonwood Lakes and the precipitous eastern escarpment of the Sierra. After more difficult and steep climbing over rocks packed with snow, he emerged on a broad and gradual shoulder less than 200 feet from the summit. Here he rested and was startled to see a giant Sierra hare bound from beneath the rocks upon which he stood and disappear over the summit. He had seen many of these big, white hares on the snows below, where they were perfectly camouflaged, but he felt it ironic that they must forage here, high on a rocky mountainside which made them quite conspicuous. He continued up the slope and within ten minutes he had reached the cairn marking the summit of Mt. Langley. He was jubilant: after five hours of hard climbing he stood atop a 14,042-foot peak, his first winter ascent to such heights.

If any earlier climber had made a winter conquest of Langley, it is unknown, and Bartholomew's diary does not mention

This unidentified snowscape met Bartholomew's lens near Army Pass.

one. Just knowing that he could reach a 14,000-foot summit at winter was all the satisfaction he sought.

The excitement of success swept all traces of earlier disappointments from his mind as he hurried to the Sierra Club register. Carefully he penciled his name and date into the small book. No other signature had been entered in the Langley register since Ed Steen's in September. Then he stepped back and observed the fantastic panorama of mountains unrolling before him, peak after peak, stacked one against the other to the distant horizons. Some of the major peaks he could identify from his earlier and easier travels. The Great Western Divide formed a great convoluted barrier above the deep trench of the Kern River Canyon running northward to a maze of distant peaks. Other natural wonders rose in the grand scene including other 14,000-foot giants with names of Tyndall, Williamson and Russell. And to the left of these monarchs, standing above all, loomed the huge, asymmetrical form of Mt. Whitney.

Finally he forced his attention from the view, moved to his pack and removed the camera. He pointed the lens in many directions, making a complete panorama from his high perch, then moved to the edge of the steep face and examined the landscape beyond. He saw a dazzling labyrinth of canyons and ridges between his position and that great peak. In addition he could see several snow-hidden lakes, including those that stair-step up through the Rock Creek Basin below. His eye ran up the length of the basin, over his unsuccessful route towards Whitney, past the Miter and on to a point hidden behind the southern ridge of Mt. McAdie.

He stood there for a long time scanning the massive maze for still another route, some access to Whitney. Many times his eye followed a possible ascent route, but on each the pathway was cut short of the summit by a ledge, a sharp ridge, a large buttress, or some other obstacle precluding further upward progress.

Bart prepares a meal at the rugged mountaineer's refuge he found on the western slopes of Whitney. This large rock and foxtail pine provided a measure of shelter when he was buffeted by fierce gale winds.

6. The Whitney Conquest

Bart returned to the crude shelter of his wickiup in high spirits. The successful climb to the top of 14,000-foot Langley had raised his hopes for another try at Mt. Whitney. While he had not spotted any route to the summit, the climb had done much more than tell him that the try for the highest mountain must be made elsewhere.

He planned to leave the Rock Creek campsite, south of Whitney, the following morning and move to the alternate assault camp on the western slopes of the mountain, but these plans were delayed until January 7 by several small storms that swept over the Sierra. Once Bart felt the storms had abated he pushed off to the north. First he dropped down to Perrin Creek, then contoured along the 10,000-foot level of the rolling forested area near Mt. Guyot. A strong wind was blowing, and as he emerged from the trees he could see great snow banners sweeping off the upper peaks.

New snow made the skiing difficult because his heavy pack pushed the skis deep into the powder, slowing his progress to less than five miles that day. But he continued the next morning along the high shelf of the Kern River Canyon and joined the snow-covered John Muir Trail at midafternoon. Bart went to the Whitney cache and was relieved to find it had not been touched by the many summer and fall visitors to the area. Nearby on an exposed southern slope he found an excellent campsite, free of snow and comfortably close to a good supply of firewood.

Settled by his campfire that evening, Bart reflected on his two weeks of solitude. He figured he had covered 35 trail miles and about twice that distance in side trips. In his diary he wrote that what most surprised him was the relatively mild weather; there had been several small storms, but eight inches was the greatest snowfall he had measured for any one day and his thermometer had not dropped below zero. All in all, he felt pleased with his progress, but noted with regret that a large part of the food in the caches would go unused, as he had needed only about a fourth of the Langley cache.

Bart rose early the next day, January 9. A hard wind was whipping his little tent ominously despite the shelter afforded by the campsite. The wind tore at his breakfast fire, whirling up billows of smoke and erratic flames. It was, he thought, an inconvenience to have his meal thus disturbed; little did he realize the wind that day would endanger his life.

While he loaded his pack and made himself ready he could see part of the great mountain. He planned to continue up Whitney Creek and prepare a base camp just above timberline from which to make his new try at Whitney's summit. He estimated the distance to be less than four miles with a rise of about 800 vertical feet.

As he set out, he knew the day would be a tough one, for the wind was swirling blankets of snow across the mountainside. Though the sky was clear, he found himself enveloped from time to time in a horizontal "snowstorm" which closed off his level vision at only a few feet. He donned goggles to keep the stinging particles from his eyes.

But as Bart climbed, his view became wider and at each rest stop more of the surrounding landscape lay revealed. At his back was the giant Kern Canyon, running straight and true,

Bart, almost at the summit of Mt. Whitney, made this late-afternoon photograph of peaks stretching away to the northwest. In foreground are the ridges of Mt. Hale; beyond, the Great Western Divide.

Pausing in his climb, Bart arranged a self-portrait with the Great Western Divide as background. This range, west of Bart's route, separates the drainages of the Kern and Kaweah rivers.

north to south. Towering above the gorge, its rugged flanks poking high into the sky, was the Great Western Divide. On his right stood the giant form of Mt. Hitchcock and beyond it the rolling, featureless country he had recently crossed. To his left rose a maze of mountains, seeming to pile one upon the other to the heavens. Directly in front was the huge bulk slanting ever upward, Whitney the challenging — never before topped by man in winter.

The wind became stronger, buffeting him at every step, forcing him to focus all his attention on the task of climbing. To him, a scene of mountain grandeur had become a picture of grimmest prospects. At times his heavy pack — which had been an anchor or a drag — became a great sail in the wind. He strained forward, each upward movement seeming to require maximum effort.

A little gully appeared and Bart stepped gratefully down into its partial protection from the wind. There he rested and had an early lunch, abbreviated to crackers, chipped beef and dried fruit to save time. He was dismayed at his lack of progress in the morning but donning a fur-lined parka from his pack, he headed again into the fury of wind.

The sky had become slightly overcast and he hoped it might signal a lessening in the force of the blow. It was not to be: the wind became stronger. But with his goal in mind he strove on, gaining only inches at times against the invisible force. Leaning, straining, he zigzagged slowly up and around ridges, seeking some momentary respite from the gale. Occasionally he rested, braced against solidly planted ski poles. Then he would go on, slowly, slowly making his way into the white hell.

The wind grew worse. The heavy canvas parka flapped violently while snow, pine needles and sand from exposed points of decomposed granite blasted him. The temperature dropped and the wind continued to gain speed, screaming about him in terrifying fury. Great chunks of frozen snow, ripped from high ridges, were hurtled down at him. Twice he was overturned by the wind and sent tumbling across the frozen surface. Sometimes great corkscrews of whipped snow would envelop him, cutting off the feeble sunlight.

Progress then became impossible: he couldn't ski, couldn't see — even standing took great effort. Never in his high mountaineering had Bart experienced such an alpine hurricane. And yet he pushed on, knowing by now that survival depended on finding some shelter where he could rest the night, for daylight was dimming by the minute. The temperature was falling but the wind continued its relentless battering.

He strained every muscle against gravity and fatigue as he moved on, hoping, praying, for some sanctuary, however slight, which would get him through the night alive. Shelter was imperative, but there was no protection here on the side of the great mountain.

Desperately he peered into the darkening surroundings: above an empty vastness, barren, gray; below the same bleakness dotted at wide intervals with a lone, gnarled tree. Then, through whipping snow, he saw a large tree braced against a boulder some seven feet high and ten feet long, big enough to afford a windbreak. This would be his campsite.

He peeled off the pack, stepped out of the skis and forced them into a crack in the rock lest they be blown away. His little tent became a flapping monster when taken from the pack, but he managed at last to get it tied to a sturdy branch of the tree and to a fallen log nearby.

Attempts to start a fire were even more frustrating. His matches would be blown out before their feeble flame could ignite the twigs he had laid as kindling; then even the twigs were blown away. Time after time he failed, but he knew that without fire for warmth and cooking he probably would not survive the night. In desperation, he took his frying pan and a handful of twigs into the tent, put the twigs in the pan and scratched a match. Slowly the flames flickered up through the tiny pieces of fuel and he added more twigs. Ignoring the smoke that seemed to fill the tent, Bart warmed his hands at the rising flame, and when the blaze reached toward the canvas of the tent he tipped the contents of the pan into the firepit just outside. The wind whipped the flames into a fury of sparks and in a sickening moment they were gone.

But a fire was a necessity; so Bart rigged a strip of canvas from his pack as a windbreak and again kindled a fire in the frying pan. This time the flames held, flashing upward through the larger sticks he had prepared. Patiently he added more wood as around and over the windbeak the wind whipped the flames through the sticks with the force of a blast furnace. Bart crouched upwind from the firepit to give the blaze a little more protection. Finally, when he felt the fire was stable he went to his pack and took out the large pot in which he would melt snow for tea. In that moment another monstrous blow came out of the night and once again the fire was whipped to oblivion.

Bart had to move quickly. He crawled to the firepit and thrust a match into the darkened, smoking ruin. Flame flashed up again. Without moving from his position, Bart sheltered the blaze as he melted snow and heated water to brew a cup of tea. It went down comfortingly warm, he found, with his hard biscuits and near-frozen chipped beef. He then anchored his water pot with a rock, crawled into the tent, wrapped himself in his down robe and slept as the night roared away outside.

The drama started in the darkness before dawn. In the high camp on Whitney's western slope, Bart awoke to find clear skies and cold air outside his little tent. The battering storm that had ravaged the mountains a day earlier had vanished. He crept upon the dark, icy stage and fixed a quick breakfast. By the gleam of the campfire he put together a light pack and made ready for the next act of his winter-long odyssey. This was January 10, 1929, the early prologue for another classic encounter between man and mountain.

Bart mounted the skis and moved out — passing over the frozen flanks of the great theater just as dawn's light outlined the gigantic form of the mountain above. The first hour went smoothly and he had climbed the lower approach to a maze of chutes that raked the west face of the giant peak. Here he was forced to remove his skis and replace them with ice creepers, which were more suited to the steep, frozen slopes. With the aid of these simple and inexpensive crampons, he climbed well up into the chutes — dragging his skis by a rope tied to his waist. He estimated that he had climbed over a thousand vertical feet when he encountered a pinnacled ridge, coated with ice and snow, intersecting the chute and barring his way to the top. Doggedly he picked his way around the point with great difficulty and managed after several minutes to clear the barrier.

Then he was moving higher again, looking skyward for the next obstacle. The chute ended under an insurmountable wall which forced him to move over a broken ridge and into a parallel gully. Soon he ran into another barrier, and several times the process of crossing from one gully to another was repeated. While he had the satisfaction of moving upward, he concluded he was lost in a labyrinth of gullies with no idea where the summit lay.

A great feeling of frustration came over Bart. He peered into the basin below, trying to find the speck which marked his camp and thus establish a reference point. He knew his original plan of veering to the north for the summit was being destroyed, but his frustration was tempered with determination and touched with an element of humor. He had often become confused about direction in a heavily forested area, he recalled, but had never thought it would happen here on the open and exposed side of a giant mountain!

He glanced up at a new overhanging wall covered with the blue opalescent, high-mountain ice and finally decided to turn southward towards nearby Mt. Muir. Carefully inching his way across another ridge, he entered a larger chute that again led upwards. His enthusiasm was renewed and he progressed easily, again on the skis which allowed him to stay on the frozen surface. The ascent in this broad chute went well at first but slowed as the slope steepened. Instead of traversing in a zigzag climb he had to sidestep up the hillside. Once his skis dislodged a large mound of frozen snow which fell far down the hill, disappearing from sight and sound. Realizing that a fall on his part would follow a similar route, he carefully unfastened the skis and replaced them with the sharp ice creepers.

By midmorning he made his first rest stop, pausing long enough to study the maps carefully. Bart estimated his position as somewhere along the 13,000-foot contour, about 1500 feet below the summit. Here the snow was thinner, undoubtedly whipped away by high winds. Yet he moved on up the chute, climbing at any agonizingly slow pace. With each upward step the route became more difficult and occasionally he had to thrust the tail of a ski into the snow — using it as a ladder rung to gain another foot or two. While such antics were helpful, Bart knew they were extremely hazardous, and any slip could be fatal.

Finally the snow disappeared completely, leaving only rock and ice beneath his feet. Footings became impossible, for below each rock lay an icy "delta" which would collapse under his weight. Noontime passed but the climbing continued, although in the thin, cold air progress was measured in inches. By midafternoon, with the sun alreay headed down the western sky, Bart stumbled upon the ice-glazed Whitney trail at an elevation of 13,600 feet.

"Six hundred feet in five hours," he gasped in disgust; he couldn't believe his snail-like progress. But with his goal in sight he moved quickly along the rocky though gentle trail. Now a new adversary — time — had signaled its challenge and he hurried on towards the crude stone cabin atop the peak. He wrote:

> Though the scramble northward along the crest of the ridge required less sustained effort, there was still much treacherous country to cross. The footing might be at one moment on a narrow ledge of ice-covered granite, the next on a wind-glazed drift. Impatient as I was to reach the summit, it seemed all obstacles known to mountaineers had been amassed to thwart progress. By the time Whitney's broad shoulder had been reached the sun was alarmingly low.

However, two weeks of high-altitude exposure had conditioned his lungs for the thin air of 14,000 feet, and he moved swiftly up along the rim of the mountain, his ski equipment flung across one shoulder.

In another hour he was there. The rocks, snow and ice, all those obstructions had disappeared. The summit was under his feet, and above him there was nothing — only the blue-black winter sky. He stopped as in a daze because he had no place to go. For a moment it seemed inconceivable that he was at last atop the highest point in the then 48 United States.

Bart hurried to the rock cairn marking the actual summit, and as he dropped his pack a feeling of euphoria overcame his weariness. Stumbling to the lip of the sheer eastern wall, he peered down into the valley miles below with all its Lilliputian objects. He stood a moment looking into space. Instead of the thrill of excitement or triumph there was a feeling of anxiety, an inclination to bolt back down the mountainside. He noted later in his diary:

> . . . but even thus fortified, how small the thrill of victory! Rather one is lost in the awe of forces and factors about him: the infinite solitude, the savage terrain, the weird dissonance of the wind. And the danger of being trapped on the mountain by darkness.

Recognizing the late hour, he spared no time to identify the major peaks and landmarks. He went quickly about his planned tasks: hanging the small recording thermometer in the shadow of the stone hut; signing the register; moving about with his camera to take several fast pictures — including three or four with the self-timer. Next he turned to making a photographic panorama of the great vista, only to discover that the camera had been improperly focused; quickly he corrected the setting and remade the pictures. Then he returned to the thermometer and noted the 26° reading.

Amid such activity he had mixed reactions touched with vague premonitions and a physical unsteadiness. Then he remembered: he hadn't eaten since breakfast, nearly nine hours earlier. He went to his bag for some biscuits and dried fruit. For a moment he rested, ever mindful of the sinking sun in the western sky. Already the long shadows were about, carrying the icy cold that numbed his hands and fingers.

His stay atop the summit was short — about twenty minutes. To delay, he knew, would invite disaster. The prospects of spending the night atop the mountain were grim and he was anxious to leave.

Bart repacked his gear and headed down the trail. He hurried along, skirting the first patchwork of snow and ice that lined his route; thoughts of trying to find his way through the maze of gullies and chutes at night urged him on. Soon he was

Although Bart's time at the summit of Whitney was extremely limited, he took a few extra minutes to set up the camera and get a shot of himself seated by the cairn, signing the register.

running back down the trail to a spot near the 14,000-foot level where he remounted his skis.

Now the adversary was *de*scent and the enemy was darkness. With all efforts concentrated on speed, Bart reached the 12,600-foot level just as the sun set behind the distant Kaweahs. Here at the head of one of many long chutes he removed the skis once more and tied them together as an improvised toboggan. With his heels hooked over the tails of the skis, he leaned forward, grasped the bindings and set off straight down the chute, praying that he had selected an unbroken gully.

He found himself propelled downward and gaining alarming speed. The walls of the chute became a blur as he schussed by. Realizing the great risk, he tried to turn off the fall line by turning the skis abruptly to the side. The maneuver sent him catapulting across the ridge and into the next chute, where he came to a grinding halt.

Miraculously, he was uninjured. To complete the descent less perilously, he put on the ice creepers and again mounted the makeshift sled. By digging the creepers' points into the frozen snow he made a slower, controlled run. The new chute turned out to be the right one, unbroken and leading to the lower slopes. He arrived back at camp an hour after dark, thankful for his safety. The casualties were his injured pride, frayed nerves and two pairs of trousers which had frozen and cracked during the impromptu descent.

7. High Winter

Early on the morning of January 11 the lone traveler skied down from his windy camp on Whitney's western slope to a white alpine basin known as Crabtree Meadow, where he found Whitney Creek open and flowing. He drank thirstily as it was his first stream water in over two weeks. After the second cup he realized how tasteless it was; compared to melted snow flavored with smoke and pine needles, this pure, sparkling water seemed flat. Normally the stream would not be flowing at midwinter, but the weather had moderated. During the night the temperature had barely dropped below freezing, and the day was surprisingly mild. By midmorning he had even shed his heavy parka.

Warm weather and poor snow is a skier's complaint and Bart could verify it. He measured the snow depth at only 18 inches and reported it wet and sticky. Over the years he had discovered that the greatest Sierra snowfall usually occurs in a belt between the elevations of 7000 and 10,000 feet. Above this, high winds, lighter snow and other climatic factors account for a shallower pack.

He had moved along the great mountainous shelf of the nearby Kern River Canyon, climbing slowly and laboriously. He called it quits shortly after noon and made camp on a bleak mountainside somewhere near the Sandy Plateau. The day's skiing had been hard and added to his fatigue, while the high journey had drained his energy. He was aware of the need of a good rest, knowing that the nights on the snow had not given him the sleep he needed to restore his strength. But on the following morning he was on his way again. Upward, towards the north he went in his accustomed ski-shuffling gait. He would rest frequently, scanning the ever-changing landscape.

For Bart it seemed as though the snow was never the same and every day produced a different surface. At times it was hardly snow but wind-swept glare ice, that made skiing difficult and sometimes hazardous. On other days the snow would be granular and so abrasive that he had to wax his skis almost hourly. And at the other end of the spectrum was the light powdery stuff in which his skies were lost from sight; in such snow Bart could scoop a handful into his mouth and find very little moisture. The most difficult surface, he found, was where several types of snow lay one atop the other, leaving large sun-cupped mounds of snow interspersed with ridges of ice. But Bart's favorite was really deep snow, though all too often he had insufficient depth for good traveling and many times he slammed against a rock or fallen branch just below the surface. The bottoms of his sturdy hickory skis were nicked and gouged by these repeated impacts.

As he contoured towards the shoulder of nearby Mt. Young he found better snow and his progress improved despite the lethargy that had touched him. He noticed that the warmer weather had brought many small animals from their winter hibernation, and he recorded their presence in his diary.

He camped the night of January 12 high on the 11,200-foot western shelf of Mt. Barnard in almost balmy weather. But it was not to last, for this was another exposed camp and he was awakened early by wind battering his tent. He poked his head out and saw ominous dark clouds moving across the canyon. Forgoing breakfast he struck camp immediately and went

Having made temporary quarters in a primitive cabin on Tyndall Creek,
Bart shed his heavy pack and parka to ski out along the stream in fair
weather.

on, hoping to find a spot more sheltered from his climatic adversary.

Prodded along by the threat in the sky, Bart moved rapidly. The mountainside, which had been alive with many birds and small animals only yesterday, was now empty. When the storm hesitated, Bart took an early lunch by a small, frozen lake. It was a place he had visited months earlier, and recalling its refreshing waters, Bart went looking for a drink. He was hungry and thirsty and felt the storm could wait until he had stoked his stomach. Scraping the snow away with the tip of a ski, he took his axe to the ice below. After 15 minutes of chopping he had cut through 18 inches of solid ice but had not reached water; so he gave up and quenched his thirst with the chipped ice.

By afternoon the clouds darkened and lowered even more. The wind rose and pushed at Bart, hurrying him along the upper reaches of the great canyon. It was a relief when he located a crude little cabin on lower Tyndall Creek. Though it was not shown on any maps, he had heard of it from other mountaineers and knew it to be an old Park Service maintenance hut. The sides, once chinked with mud, showed many holes while the one window was broken and snow had drifted in around the open door. Primitive as it was, he welcomed its shelter from the impending storm. He built a fire on the dirt floor where a hole in the roof would serve as a smoke vent, then scraped and pitched out most of the snow and settled down for the storm.

He slept well that night; the mattress of earth offered comfort a bed laid on snow could not provide. He was awakened once by the sound of small animals scurrying through his pack, looking for food. He got up and hung the food bags from nails in the roof beams. By morning the wind and snow had passed and Bart set up serious housekeeping after breakfast was finished. During the night he had decided to lay over here for a

High on the slopes of 14,000-foot Mt. Tyndall, Bartholomew watches a storm approach the Diamond Mesa and Junction Peak. During the middle week of January 1929 a series of hard storms swept the high country.

One of nearly 400
photographs Bart made
during the expedition,
this view of Kern Ridge
from above Tyndall
Creek shows his skill
with the camera
equipment of the day.

few days and rest; so he cleaned and straightened the cabin as best he could, warmed water and enjoyed a "bucket bath," his first bath in nearly three weeks. He also made some needed repairs to his clothing and other equipment which were showing the wear and tear of the journey. When the weather kept him inside Bart spent some of his time writing the details of his previous observations.

In better weather he made several extensive day trips unencumbered by the usual, heavy pack. One of these took him far up the slopes of another 14,000-foot giant, Mt. Tyndall. As he neared the top of an upper ridge a storm swept in over the neighboring peaks, and Bart set about taking picture after picture. The towering background provided superb, snow-covered landscapes, and for some of the exposures he used the self-timer attachment so he could be seen in the foreground.

Before the weather forced him down the mountainside he had exposed two more rolls of film. Since the start of his trip 18 rolls had been exposed, and carefully packed away for the detour he would take by way of Kearsarge Pass to the town of Independence. Bart knew he was making the first pictures of the Sierra winter; he well understood the pitfalls of winter photography in the mountains and he hoped he had avoided them. When he used the self-timer the gale-like winds would jar the camera; so he tied a rock to it or set rocks against its slender frame. And when the shutter was frozen or choked with snow he learned to estimate how much its timing was delayed.

During the week Bart eventually spent at the cabin he made two trips to the nearby cache. He ate well as the cache held ample food — more than he ever could use. He regretted that Ed Steen was not with him, sharing the supplies and the high scenery.

At one point it seemed to Bart that he had been in the mountains forever. Weeks had gone by since he had seen another person, and the days had fused into one long and lonely season of cold and wind, snow and ice. Had it not been for the daily diary entry, he would have lost track of the day of the week and the month.

These notations gave him great satisfaction, for each represented another day of solitary, high-mountain survival. Much of the information he recorded was semi-scientific. Each day's entry included the facts of the weather—the minimum and maximum temperatures, the appearance of the sky and the "feel" and direction of the wind. He had not been able to find a wind gauge which would fit in his pack and so could only estimate wind speeds.

On January 14 he noted a balmy high temperature of 47°, but usually his maximum temperatures were below freezing. Once Bart doubted the accuracy of his minimum reading, because he had recorded only one that was below zero even though to him many early mornings had seemed to be much colder. Many of the readings were two degrees above zero, and Bart wondered if the instrument were somehow faulty.

Temperatures, sky cover and the like are real things and Bart could record them, but there were other phenomena that lonely winter less amenable to his reporting, even though his sensory system was well tuned to the mountains. Sounds were among them and occasionally he put them down in the little diary. He mentioned the thunderous roar of an avalanche ripping down a steep canyon, the lonely wail of a coyote, the distinctive howl of wolves (long considered to be extinct in the Sierra). Some new sounds he took no note of — the real and routine effects of a man making a journey where no man should be at that season of the year. The first crackling of his morning campfire, the ring and clatter of his few utensils as he prepared breakfast and the noises of breaking camp all seemed quite unimportant. So were the creaking sounds of his ski bindings, the rhythmic crunching of skis on new snow, the heavy breathing from long, hard climbs and the swishing sound of skis gliding down long slopes. But there were other sounds: during the cold nights the temperature dropped until even the trees protested with bark splitting and breaking; and on one night during that week he saw and heard a meteorite impact far down the Kern River Canyon.

And then there was the unaccountable sensation that some call the "sound of silence" while others identify as the solitary sound of loneliness. It could be the inner vibration of life, the harmonics of one's own body, but whatever it may be, it is a strange experience born of man, mind and mystery in the high mountains. And at times it is almost a visible sound. Bartholomew knew this phenomenon, might feel it as he scanned the high ridges and searched the deep canyons, looking, listening. At times he strained for it, waited for it and felt it. During the long 13- and 14-hour winter nights he was most aware of the sensation; as darkness fell around his evening campfire he would look into the inky blackness beyond the flames, seeking something, someone — the unknown. Even after he had crawled into his little tent he would hear the sound, compounded and amplified as a seashell does the pulse in the ear. Bart called it the "sound of nothing," but it was the seemingly audible reminder that except for the mountains and the stars he was alone . . . all alone.

Many times there were the sounds and sensations that go with frustration and failure: twice that week he had been forced off the approach to Harrison Pass by furious storms. This pass reaches an elevation of 12,600 feet, its knife-edged summit separating the Kings and Kern River drainages with high peaks. Bart had never tested its slopes before, even in summer, but undoubtedly his hazardous crossing on an alternate route, Shepherd Pass, during the summer trip had convinced him this high divide had to be crossed here.

Thus on January 21, after two prior attempts, he was headed for Harrison again, having left camp in the deep darkness before dawn and made his way to timberline just as the first light of morning crept onto the bleak mountainside. Except for two large Sierra hares which ran for cover, the icy landscape was stark and empty. Overhead was his high battleground, shrouded in clouds and ravaged by winds that signaled yet another storm. Giant snow plumes were wheeling off the higher peaks, and often underfoot he would encounter new snow, transferred here by the raging blow from peaks and passes where it had first fallen.

As he left the protection of the few trees that marked timberline he was hit by the full force of the winds. They seemed to be of gale strength, perhaps more savage than those he had encountered two weeks before near Whitney Creek. Snow, pine needles, anything that would move with the winds, including dirt and dust from the snow-free areas, blasted his face. The weight of his seventy-pound pack seemed at times a useful anchor, holding the gale in check.

It was midmorning before he reached the 12,000-foot level, near the snowbound basin marking South America Lake. Soon thereafter the clouds lowered and it started snowing again. The enveloping weather and its white-out effect limited his vision to a few hundred feet and created some confusion about the right direction to the pass.

That day would have discouraged anyone, and even Bart sensed defeat under these conditions. From the crest of the pass the wind now tore cakes of crusted snow, hurling them down the mountainside. The formidable missiles all seemed to miss him; so he continued the assault, although at times he was

Gnarled foxtail pines show that the wind blows from the west on the Bighorn Plateau.

forced to turn his face from the fury of the snow-and-ice-carry-
ing wind roaring down. Once again the mountain seemed to
fight him, but before he would consider any retreat he was determined to top the pass and reconnoiter the far side.

About three hundred feet from the top Bart gained the protection of two larger boulders that jutted from the slope. Here
he rested, as the effects of the altitude, the battering wind and
the climb were making themselves felt. He removed his pack
and examined the map; wool liners were added to the mittens
and the parka hood was drawn tighter. Then he moved on.

He had climbed only a short distance when he entered an
area of comparative calm. While the storm roared over the
pass, here under the lip of a large overhanging snow cornice it
was relatively still, giving Bart an opportunity to exchange his
skis for ice creepers. Again the skis were tied to his belt with
a small strap, and with the use of ski poles and axe he finally
clawed into the turmoil on the pass. Carefully he crawled over
the knife-edge of the pass and looked down. He recoiled in
dismay: a vertical chasm, its upper flank a 300-foot precipice,
yawned below him.

Was the map wrong? Had he climbed the wrong col?

A trail crossed the pass — that was what the map showed,
but any kind of a trail here was impossible. A long scanning of
the area failed to reveal any avenue of descent. Bart's usual
optimism ebbed and he lay there a long time.

Then the wind and the cold roused him. To remain would
be disastrous; to move was imperative. He could retreat, yield
his hard-won elevation and return to Tyndall Creek and a measure of safety and comfort, but he resisted.

He looked over the sheer face again and shuddered, then
began creeping eastward. Surely there must be a way down
somewhere. After 500 feet of crawling he came to what appeared to be a long snow chute but was guarded by a huge

buttress of rock so that he could not see its upper slope. Inching his way around the great rock, he peered down from its other side to find the chute broken by an impossible drop a little way down from its top. However, from here he could see what might be another chute; so he crawled and struggled back to the knife-edge and crept along it for a better view. It was a clear chute, a steep but unbroken slope ending in a cirque far below. He had a way down, if he could get onto it.

The top was blocked by a wind-built, 15-foot cornice of snow and ice. Bart inched his way to the edge of the protruding lip to study it; finally he concluded that the only way to get down to the chute would be to cut into the cornice, which would be perilous as the snow of the curl's underside was much softer than the crusted top. Drawing his ax from the pack, taking care to make no sudden move that would jeopardize his delicate foothold, he began cutting into the lip. The snow blocks that he chopped away burst into a thousand pieces as they hit below. Carefully he leaned out from the edge and made repeated blows at the cornice's soft underbelly. The freezing winds plucked at him, and each swing of the ax required some contorted position. Then he jammed a ski pole into the harder snow and leaned on it to extend his downward reach. Finally he had a snowy niche into which he committed his body, spread-eagled against the snow, setting his pole to support his weight and testing its hold before reaching downward to do more chopping. The weight of his pack tugged outward as he worked, and he had to force from his mind the thoughts of an icy death awaiting below.

Half an hour of leaning, chopping, testing and inching downward time and again brought him to the head of the chute but the battle was not over. The chute turned out to be a ribbon of ice covered by about three inches of new snow which quickly caked his ice creepers so that he had to clean them for

Bartholomew took refuge in this crude cabin on Tyndall Creek in mid January 1929, spending a week exploring the winter isolation of the High Sierra.

almost every step. Even with the creepers biting into the underlying ice, the going was hazardous and in most places Bart axed out foothold after foothold in a zigzag course down the steep descent — chop, careful step, chop again.

At midafternoon he was barely halfway down — he could hardly believe he had come such a short distance with so much effort. He knew he was tiring and the mental and physical strain of the day was slowing him down. But the prospect of a night on such terrain left him no alternative but to reach safety before relaxing.

Then the weather relented as wind and snow which had battered him subsided. Over the high spires of Mt. Brewer, Bart could see patches of blue working upward in the western sky. The sight seemed to give him new strength and he chopped and hacked his way along until at last, as he reached the bottom of the chute, the sun broke through the wild clouds for a brief moment, then dipped behind the mountains.

Darkness was only an hour away and Bart figured he was again just below 12,000 feet in elevation. Timberline, where fuel could be had, was still 2000 feet of vertical descent and much more than that in distance away. But now he was on skiing snow, in places good skiing snow, and he headed toward the lower lip of the moraine which lay at the bottom of the chute. Trouble overtook him again as he discovered that below that moraine lay an intricate mass of smaller moraines — a labyrinth of rocky banks that forced him to make wide detours. He stumbled and fell several times as his skis encountered the talus mounds hidden by the snow, but at last he found a smooth slope dropping away to timberline.

He pointed his skis down and in a few minutes was in a clump of pines. He had stomped a platform in the snow just as darkness rang down the curtain. It was no luxury resort but there were pine boughs for a bed and fire, and Bart put them to good use. Just before he rolled into his tent he pulled his thermometer from its case in his pack: two degrees above zero again.

"Altogether, a perfect evening," he wrote in his diary.

Atop Glen Pass, Bart scrounged enough firewood to prepare a needed lunch. Just minutes before, he had escaped an avalanche of the unsettled new snow on the south slope of the pass.

8. Up and Down the Mountain Slide

Three weeks later near Glen Pass north of Charlotte Lake, Bart began playing hide and seek with an unknown winter traveler. For weeks now he had made careful observations of the many telltale tracks that the year-round residents of the Sierra had left imprinted in the snow. Sometimes the tracks were ill-defined or even obscured by the ever-changing snows; here, however, there were many clean and distinct footprints, including one Bart had not seen for many years. He studied these new prints for a long time before concluding that they belonged to a large wolverine.

Even in 1929, wolverines were rare in the Sierra. While Bart had observed them years ago, this was his first sight of the tracks of the medium-sized animal with a reputation for fearlessness and fighting ability. The wolverine and the California bighorn sheep were close to joining the California grizzly bear in extinction, and Bart was pleased to see these tracks. He even took time to photograph the trail, although hampered by the flat lighting that produced little or no definition.

Since they were both headed towards Glen Pass, Bart entered the chase in hopes of gaining a glimpse of his fellow traveler. The game took on increased dimension on the lower approaches of the pass when Bart discovered newer and even larger tracks. These were patterned similar to those of a coyote but were twice as large and with a longer stride between paw prints. They too headed up the pass.

Against a panorama of snowy peaks, Bart's skis and pack rest in the saddle of 11,800-foot Kearsarge Pass. The mountain traveler crossed here twice during a planned detour to Independence, where he mailed films and reports to an associate in Big Creek.

From his Alaskan travels Bart immediately recognized them as wolf prints. While he had heard what he believed to be wolf calls in Kern River Canyon, these tracks were the first he had ever seen in the Sierra, and they apparently disproved some authorities who had never recognized the presence of wolves in this range. Figuring he might see at least one of the strangers, Bart continued up the mountainside. Finding the tracks had dismissed the apprehension he felt about crossing Glen Pass, for even in summer this Sierra crest was difficult and dangerous.

He moved steadily up the slope, glancing occasionally skyward to the steep and snow-heavy ridges above. The ascent began in long traverses with kick turns that headed him off on a reciprocal angle — an otherwise zigzag trail up the flanks of the mountainside. Towards the top and about 300 feet below the saddle that marked the pass Bart rested, panting against the strain of the climb. Thoughts of animal tracks were swept from his mind as he examined the view ahead: the steep hillside fresh with new snow looked dangerous. A premonition of trouble perturbed him as he observed the steep slopes above, dotted with rocks and ridges.

As he approached one of these obstacles he heard something, almost like a cracking sound. In an instant he was ripped from the slope and sent tumbling down the mountainside. But instinctively, as if directed by some innate power, he struggled atop the avalanche. Clouds of snow swirled about him. It seemed like an eternity, but in a moment he had stopped sliding, cast aside as the main body of the avalanche continued down the hillside. Carefully he rose to his skis, taking every precaution not to start another slide. He was greatly relieved to find himself intact, with his sole casualty a ski pole strap.

His pack had been wrenched to the side of his body; he straightened this and was soon climbing, amazed that he only

Bart gets a meal going on
a small fire at camp near
Mather Pass. On 42
nights he bivouacked
above 10,000 feet in
elevation.

had fallen less than a hundred feet. As he regained the lost distance he noticed more snow and rocks sliding off the hillside and knew that the chance for another, even more severe avalanche was imminent. He carefully removed his skis and started kicking footsteps into the snow. It was a difficult and laborious process, but one he felt was safer than traversing under the cliff above. Soon the ascent became more difficult, requiring Bart to thrust the heels of his skis into the steep slope and use them as a mountain climber might use ice picks. It was an extremely slow means of travel, but eventually he caterpillared his way onto the pass.

Once atop the gap he rested. Before heading down the north slope to the Rae Lakes basin, he scouted the pass and found the two tracks he had been chasing. The wolverine evidently knew the country well, including the trail; the other winter traveler had followed the route of the snow-covered trail, avoiding it only where rocks or snow had fallen across it. As Bart moved down the mountainside the wolf tracks disappeared, and the wolverine evidently added to his lead by backing down the steep slopes, using his front paws as brakes. By cutting across the switchback the animal had set a direct course for the little ridge that bisects one of the lakes. Bart abandoned the chase here and made camp in the basin. On the following morning he moved down to the nearby food cache, spotting the wolverine tracks again. Bart concluded that the carnivore didn't care much for porcupines since he had passed within a few yards of two without bothering either.

Next morning, February 13, Bart made another of his frequent side trips into the upper end of the circque holding Dragon Lake, taking several photographs en route. Along the way he heard the distinctive call of the nuthatch — another first sighting of a bird whose habitat is usually much lower in elevation, especially in winter. He returned to camp early having

Looking west across the saddle of Mather Pass, Bart's camera picks out his pack and skis just at the wind-sculptured edge. His ski trail leading up from the south and the individual footprints toward his vantage point can be traced in this photograph.

spotted a water ouzel, Sierra hares, marten and a porcupine. That afternoon, while preparing dinner, he heard the sound of rock and snow slides throughout the basin. On the next morning he left camp early, and skiing past Fin Dome he ran across another porcupine. He spent over an hour taking several pictures of the spiny creature, then arrived at the mouth of the South Fork of Woods Creek about noon.

While he prepared lunch it clouded over. Figuring he was in for a snowstorm, Bart fixed up a camp only to see it clear shortly thereafter. Rather than go through all the motions of packing again, he settled there for the day, making a short swing through the country where he observed and recorded the presence of more fauna.

Bart's game of hide and seek with the wolverine ended in a tie on February 15. As he skied across the Woods Creek basin the snow improved and he made excellent time. Just as he was starting along the northern fork of Woods Creek he spotted his elusive friend on the other side of the river, bounding through the heavy snows at a rate much slower than Bart's. For Bart the long-delayed meeting was anticlimactical: this animal was much smaller than he expected, and only twice as large as a porcupine. Bart reflected that the wolverine had a unique configuration making it about ninety percent feet and ten percent body. He considered crossing the riverbed and photographing the animal, but when he figured the extra work required to cross the gully against the small photographic prize, he terminated the cat and mouse game right there.

Throughout the rest of the daylight hours Bart observed more and more animal life. Two miles below Woods Lake he heard the drumming sound of grouse and the barking of many conies. Camp was set under the sprawling canopy of a whitebark pine tree near Twin Lakes. The weather had remained clear and calm, with no measurable snowfall in over a week.

This fact was especially evident the next morning as Bart pulled towards 12,000-foot Pinchot Pass: the south-facing slope was pockmarked with rocks and other obstructions, and in many places the edge of the trail lay exposed above the snowline. Aside from this minor problem, the climb to Pinchot Pass was easily achieved.

He found the top of the pass windblown with only a foot of snow trying to cover the rocky col. As it was nearing lunchtime, he made a small campfire from twigs and brush that pushed their struggling arms above the snow. While the soup was heating he unpacked his camera and made a dozen exposures from this high and lonely viewpoint; several were taken with the self-timer as Bart posed around the smoking campfire. In all, the lunch period was a short moment of pleasure, breaking the long period of dull climbing to the high pass. Stretching before and behind him as far as he could see lay a vast array of canyons, broken only by a mighty maze of mountain peaks. From the memorable scene to the south he searched for his lofty alpine friends. Langley, Whitney, and Tyndall were no longer identifiable; despite their 14,000-foot heights they had become lost in a jutting mass of white pyramids. Even the closer mountains guarding Harrison Pass had been blocked from sight by other snowclad peaks.

Bart gazed at the huge panorama for a long time, wondering and questioning the very origin of these gigantic forms, but finishing lunch he readied his pack and set northward. As he dropped down he came across better snow in the sheltered and protected north-facing basin. In a few minutes he reached the east rim of Marjorie Lake that lies in the cirque below the pass. An abstract pattern of glare ice ran across its frozen surface, the snow having been blown off by earlier winds. From there he reached out onto the broad, undulating slopes that led to the canyon floor and the South Fork of the Kings River.

After crossing Mather Pass the lone mountaineer came upon the Palisade group of 14,000-foot peaks. Near here he encountered a series of ice avalanches.

Contouring just above the valley floor he skied for the Cardinal cache and an old cabin nearby. He went first to the cache and was relieved to find it all right, for he had placed the supplies earlier when deer hunters were still in the area and had been concerned for its safety. Not only did he find it safe, but the hunters had left additional supplies, some of which were badly ravaged by mice and marmots. Bart was to spend three very enjoyable days in the old cabin. On the first morning he attended to the accumulated domestic duties of washing and woodgathering, plus making some needed repairs on his skiing equipment. The once-fine ski edges had become a mass of splinters; their lacquered bottoms had long since been skied away. The worn ski surfaces communicated a strange story of travel that only cross-country skiers would understand. Luckily the bindings were intact.

In the afternoon he returned to his skis and headed up toward Upper Basin for a short side trip. Although the weather had deteriorated he moved high onto the shoulder of Mt. Ruskin to inspect the surrounding mountainside, for he was especially anxious to view the approach to Mather Pass, an area unfamiliar to the lone traveler and the next leg of his long journey.

He completed the short jaunt in a few hours and now realized he would have a steep climb to the next pass. On his return he discovered several large wolf tracks below his cabin. Bart carefully inspected the new prints, and concluded that the hut had been visited by more than one wolf. He had heard their lonely wail weeks earlier and had seen their tracks atop Glen Pass; so he was assured that the Sierra wolf was not extinct. No other subjective or emotional comment was made of these tracks; and nowhere else in his winter-long travel did Bartholomew ever again see or hear an indication of this Sierra enigma.

Before Bart reached Mather Pass he spent three quiet days in this snug old cabin near the South Fork of the Kings River. Through the trees to the right can be seen the pointed summit of Arrow Peak.

The following morning dawned gray and stormy, snowing lightly all day. It delayed Bart's departure until February 19, when the locomotion process began again. Despite the new snow and the climbing, he moved upward in his approach to another untried pass. By midafternoon he had made camp at a location nearly three miles below Mather Pass, at the upper edge of timberline.

There is nothing in Bartholomew's diary to explain why he attempted 12,000-foot Mather Pass in winter. In a decade of mountain rambling he had never tried this steep approach which leads from the south into the huge basin of the Middle Fork of the Kings River. It lay beyond the range of his earlier winter explorations, and during the summer trips he had avoided the pass because it was difficult if not impassable for stock.

The adjoining basin is a rugged chaos of canyons and gorges rimmed with great peaks. The streams which drain it have carved one of the deepest canyons in the world, the Kings River Canyon, containing the most inaccessible geography in California, for the approaches to this huge area are through passes of dizzying height. Understandably the exploration of this basin was limited to such hardy explorers as John Muir and B. C. Brown until the 20th century. Even the California Indians avoided the region, preferring other passes to the north and south. The early Spanish explorers who named the Kings River, which here springs forth as a stream, made no visits to these great headwaters.

An easier, lower pass several miles to the west, Cartridge Pass, was familiar to Bartholomew and should have seemed more attractive, but it was over Mather that he pointed his skis.

The long climb up the south slope, on February 20 was relatively easy, he found, and he was able to use his skis until within 100 feet of the top. Once there he was rewarded by superb views in all directions. The fantastically sculptured white landscape cried out for recording and he photographed more than twenty views from his high vantage point.

Then he started down the north slope and into the deep canyon. He was surprised to find the way no steeper than the side he had ascended. Recent storms had covered most of the obstructions and he made good progress in the ideal weather, clear and calm. The combination allowed Bart the luxury of feeling that things at last were going his way.

At noon he ate a cold lunch — reporting he could find no firewood nor a suitable place for a fire — on the broad ledge that held the frozen lakes of upper Palisade Creek. The springlike weather — 50° at noon — encouraged him to relax and stretch out against his pack, enjoying the sun and studying the contour map of the area. He figured he could easily make the few miles to Deer Meadow by midafternoon.

But the snow that had been firm and smooth became wet and heavy in the afternoon sun and the going became difficult even before he entered a steep area of broken cliffs and ridges that dropped away sharply to the canyon floor. Soon a narrow, secondary canyon seemed to envelop him and closed off from his view the reference points he needed for direction. He felt that only gravity knew the way through this labyrinth, and its course was much too steep and dangerous to follow directly. For nearly two hours he struggled downward, lost in the vast whiteness except that for direction he could take the shadow creeping up the far wall of the canyon. The heavy snow became impossible to ski and his progress was limited to side-slipping steps. Gone was his earlier sense of well being, for the day had turned to despair.

And then it happened — a crack like the report of a distant cannon. Bart recognized it as the breaking-away sound of an avalanche, somewhere up-canyon from him and out of sight.

He was safe from that one, he knew, but the threat of others in the heavily snow-covered slopes above him was enforced by the thunder of another and nearer slide. Then there was another and another, each seeming to be closer and louder than the one before it.

Bart was scanning his immediate area for a buttress or promontory that would offer him some protection when a thunderous roar came from directly across the canyon. Bart watched spellbound as nature's awesome force transfigured the canyon wall. He realized that what he had assumed to be snowslides were avalanches of slab ice. Huge sheets of ice and frozen snow, loosened by the warming sun, crashed off the mountainside and in turn triggered secondary slides of snow and rock which ripped on down the slope in one of nature's great face liftings.

With new understanding he looked at the high slope above him and recognized, glistening in the sun, the dangerously heavy sheets of ice interspersed in the snowfields. There was nothing to do but get away from there if he could, and he renewed his slow descent to the echoing roar of more avalanches. The afternoon was still warming.

Suddenly a slope a hundred yards behind him, one he had just crossed, let go in a crash of monumental sound. Bart stood transfixed: huge sheets of ice and snow ripped loose and crashed down the mountainside. The snow and rocks, he wrote later, took the short route of gravitational force but the great sheets of ice became airborne and tossed and turned in acrobatic dives.

For nearly two hours he made his way down toward the valley floor, escaping by sheer fortune the death-dealing sweep of the avalanches. Several times deep cuts of his skis triggered small slides. On one occasion he was showered with slivers of ice as a gliding sheet crashed nearby.

There was no relief when he reached the narrow floor of the upper canyon, for here he was exposed to falls of ice and snow from either side. He pushed on hurriedly. In his experience of winter mountaineering he could not recall the desperation that he knew now, but he was able to grin for a moment at his classical mountain situation — that of being in the wrong place at the wrong time.

Then he reasoned out a plan of survival: he would ski as fast as he could until he came to the base of a spent avalanche and there he would rest, safe, he felt, because the snows above this spot had already come crashing down. Even so, sheets of ice sometimes swished over his head as he skied with all his strength from one haven to another. The double strain of intense physical effort and mental stress began to tell. He fell several times and occasionally plowed into blocks of ice or frozen snow which he would have avoided easily in better circumstances. It was nearly dark when he reached the safety of Deer Meadow. Nearly exhausted, he doffed his pack and set up camp in a clump of trees. While eating a simple meal he reflected on the day which had started so auspiciously: he had climbed 2000 feet to the top of Mather Pass, skied around some there to take his pictures from the most advantageous spots and then begun in high spirits the descent of Palisade Creek — 3000 desperate feet and ten of the most difficult miles he had ever skied.

Bart was awakened in the night by new avalanches crashing down the canyon walls but knew he was out of their reach. He resolved he would go on. Detours and delays he expected; death or disaster he could face again, but defeat he would not accept.

He was up at 4 a.m. and recorded the weather as clear, calm and cold; above the canyon walls he could see a million stars. The snow had firmed in the night's cold and Bart hurried to get

HIGH ODYSSEY

out on it. By dawn he was skiing along Palisade Creek, flowing here between iced and snowy rocks. He intended to make Grouse Meadows by evening.

By midmorning he entered an even wider part of the canyon; the sun was warm and many denizens of the area were abroad. Bart took off his parka and made a few pictures. His diary reveals he saw Douglas squirrels, marten, nutcrackers and chickadees, a lone coyote and the tracks of a weasel. Originally he had planned for a longer stay along Palisade Creek but the threat of avalanches kept him moving. He reached Grouse Meadows near the confluence of the creek and the Kings River shortly after noon. There he lunched and rested until the snow began to firm in late afternoon and he pushed off again, headed for another mountain valley, Little Pete Meadow.

· 118 ·

9. Detours and Delays

All of Bart's winter travel was characterized by deviations from the direct route, for he avoided, when he could, the most perilous paths, the snow-scarce slopes and the precipitous drops. But he planned two major detours as well, and both took him into the Owens Valley.

His precious photographic negatives were Bart's first concern, because he knew the hazards of the journey ahead and thought it unwise to carry the exposed film longer than necessary. From Independence he would mail it to Bob Parker at Big Creek, and he hoped that when he reached Bishop he would have word of the quality of his work. Also, he would send letters to family and friends who of course had received no news of him in a month.

So it was on January 26, after his crossing of knife-edged Harrison Pass, that he had left his camp near East Lake, reached down toward Bubbs Creek, dropped below Bullfrog Lake in a severe snowstorm, then crossed Kearsarge Pass and skied down Onion Valley to Independence. There he had bought toothpaste and replaced his lost pocketknife and badly worn mittens and trousers. Two days later he had been back in the high country and headed for Glen Pass.

It was almost a month later and many miles farther north when Bart climbed out of the deep recess of LeConte Canyon and headed off the crest trail toward Bishop. The way was to

The camera with its self-timer catches Bart studying a map and comparing it with the majestic terrain near Mather Pass. He is not lost, but avalanche dangers in the pass have made him seek another route.

take him upward 4000 feet to the saddle of Bishop Pass, no difficult crossing in summer but in winter it is different. As Bart reached a place where he could see the top of the pass he noted a great snow cornice hanging on a high rim just east and above the saddle. The huge white lip seemed to hang at a dangerous angle, carved by the wind into a protruding shelf that teetered on the brink of crashing into the pass below. When he moved in for a closer view, Bart recalled his terrible experience in the ice avalanches along Palisade Creek two days before.

This seemed not the time to tempt fate again and he left his chosen route to head off toward the Inconsolable Range, a rugged spur of the 14,000-foot Palisade group. "A detour from a detour," he called this trip, and he was pleased to find excellent snow as he skied past Saddlerock and Long Lakes. Soon he was at South Lake enjoying the hospitality of two old friends, Mr. and Mrs. Rose (no relation to the author), the winterbound caretakers at the Southern Sierra Power Company's plant there. He spent the night with them and skied down toward Bishop Creek in the morning.

Alerted by a phone call from Rose, W. B. Parcher, who was the Bishop newspaper editor and an old friend of Bart, met him at snowline and took him into the little community east of the range. Bearded and long-haired, Bart wrote one of his friends that he was shocked by his appearance when he first looked in a mirror.

Several letters awaited him in Bishop; many townspeople came to see Bart who was astounded by his fame. In three days he wrote many letters, sent off some more film to Bob Parker, and just before his departure on February 27 received a heartening telegram from Parker telling that the films dispatched from Independence had been developed and were excellent. With that news and a royal sendoff from the people of Bishop he headed back into the high country in fine spirits.

Returning from the detour to Bishop, Bart found skiing conditions in LeConte Canyon had deteriorated. The high daytime temperatures are best illustrated by the way he stands on this snow-free ridge, his shirt cuffs and collar unbuttoned.

On March 1 he crossed Bishop Pass after he found that the giant cornice of snow has disappeared, making it safe to follow the easier, usual route. He dropped down into Dusy Basin with affectionate memories of Bishop and a parcel of home-cooked food Mrs. Rose had given him when he visited them on the return trek.

Food was on his mind when he discovered that a marten had made free with the provisions he had left at one of his campsites. However, it was only a short trip to the Palisade cache, where he loaded into his pack all he would need until the next can along the route. It was at the Palisade cache that Bart solved the mystery of the unusual flavor in some of his meals. The moment he lifted the lid of the cache the riddle was answered. His diary entry reminded:

. . . soap will hereafter be excluded from the big can. Mush de wisteria. Hotcakes de lilac. Whew! Taste the smell.

But it was not all fun and games. On the eastern slope of LeConte Canyon he found poor snow, eroded by constant wind and softened by daytime temperatures near 50°. Going down the steep canyon side the next morning, he experienced growing difficulty on the icy crust which overlay the mushy snow. As the crust softened in the rising temperature it began breaking under his skis, which crunched onto hidden rocks and logs. Fearing he would break his neck or one of his skis, he stopped and made camp just above Little Pete Meadow.

He started early the next morning, heading for Muir Pass on snow still firm from the night's freeze, but he noted the streams were flowing, and by midmorning Bart heard the first of a series of avalanches crashing into the canyon. At noon the snow was soft and the going hard. At times it seemed to Bart he was always climbing. His descents from the high passes usually had been quick and easy but this uphill slope required an eternity of effort. The climb to Muir Pass was no exception: about 4000 feet in elevation lay before his ski tips and the slushy snow held him back. Bart knew the trail distance from the bottom of the canyon to the top of the pass was about eight miles but felt he had covered that distance already in zigzag climbing and slipping and sliding. By midafternoon the snow was too mushy to travel and so he made camp. That evening he reckoned up his ascents and figured he had topped 60,000 vertical feet since beginning the journey at Lone Pine.

The camp was below Helen Lake and he left it early the next day to continue the climb. Above timberline he noted the animal tracks he had been seeing lower down were absent. The snow depth increased, but still the going was arduous and he was feeling deep fatigue until, finally, he saw the familiar saddle of Muir. In a burst of energy he climbed quickly to the simple rock cairn that marked the top of the pass.

It was nearly noon and a great panorama of familiar scenes was unrolled before him. He doffed the pack, got out his camera and took picture after picture in the grip of a great nostalgia, for here was his own backyard. The Kings River drainage was behind him; ahead were great peaks he could identify as old friends. The evolutionist Darwin, the biologist Haeckel, and the philosopher Spencer all were honored in the names of mountains he could see from the pass. And even from this distance he could name the lakes below and remember a dozen earlier visits to their shores.

He went to the register in the cairn to enter his name and the date, March 4; the page revealed that no one had passed this way since early October. He lunched on hard biscuit, chipped beef and some walnuts in the packet Mrs. Rose had given him. While he ate, he studied in detail the area over which he would have to descend to reach timberline at the far end of Evolution Lake: the snow was broken and crusted; the

Bart reached the midpoint of his winter-long odyssey at Muir Pass, elevation 12,050 feet. Here the rugged explorer signs the register. Light snows and strong winds have exposed many rocks, which caused him great difficulty.

The above photograph of sunset at Dusy Basin, taken from near the Palisades cache, shows Bart's travel conditions: thin, crusted snow blown away
from rocks and ground vegetation. In contrast, the picture below was taken
during a different winter trip to the Evolution Basin when a thick, white
mantle made skiing easy.

lakes were frozen and swept clear of snow. Behind them was Mt. McGee and, behind it, a continuous ridge appropriately known as Glacier Divide.

Soon Bart set a downward course for Evolution Basin, knowing as he did so the going would be rough at best. The previous winter, he recalled, he had skied the five miles from the pass to the outlet of Evolution Lake in less than an hour. Now he struggled more than four hours and was still short of his goal. He fell several times as his skis bounced and skidded through the sun-cupped snowfields, almost out of control. In the next minute, it seemed, one or both of them would crash through the undermined crust. During the descent he painfully twisted his ankle in the worst fall he had sustained.

When he broke through the snow and fell into the stream below Sapphire Lake, he removed the skis in disgust and slogged and waded the remaining distance to his selected campsite on foot. He was, he wrote in his diary that evening, much the worse for wear: wet, tired and sunburned, discouraged and nursing what seemed to be a sprained ankle. This was the only time in the diary that he complains of discomfort. A sprained ankle could have doomed him, but after a day of rest the pain lessened considerably. Soon the joint was strong and bothered him not at all.

Mild temperatures and bright sun seemed to be bringing an early spring to the mountains and by March 7 Bart was "grounded" in the area below Evolution Valley: rocks and bare ground made skiing impossible. For a little way he found and traveled a sort of snow network in the shaded places, but it soon ran out. As an old snow gauger, he estimated the ground cover at less than thirty percent of normal. A year before, he and Sam Griggs had skied through here over snow so deep it covered almost everything; now every rock, bush and bank was exposed.

Near Evolution Valley this porcupine perched in a tree allowed Bartholomew to make a dozen pictures. Bart's winter expedition revealed an amazingly active animal life in the snow-covered Sierra.

Bart could hardly believe that winter was over. In normal years, he knew, the greatest snow depth in the high country occurred in late March. However, the weather was unsettled and perhaps a good storm would materialize.

He spent March 8 in camp studying his alternatives. He could end the expedition there, dropping down to Florence Lake and thence to civilization; he could slog along his planned route on foot, hoping for a storm; or he could hike out to Camp 62, about twenty miles toward Florence Lake, and borrow a pair of snowshoes which would get him over the slushy snow better than either skis or boots. The next morning brought a clear sky and a northwest wind, conditions Bart knew did not preface a storm; so he shouldered his skis and headed toward Camp 62, the Southern California Edison Company's big construction camp and Bart's second home.

He was beginning to believe this was the end of winter. As he strode down the trail he noted many birds and small animals seemingly celebrating the arrival of spring, and the creeks and rivers were running high. Below the confluence of Piute Creek and the San Joaquin River he found the trail free of snow.

At Camp 62, Bart was warmly welcomed by close friends and former co-workers. He bunked in Sam Griggs' cabin and enjoyed the luxury of a bed, a bath, and Mrs. Griggs' cooking. Sam arrived from Big Creek late that night, bringing about 15 pounds of mail for Bart, whom he characterized as his "famous friend who could carry anything except his own fan mail." It was Griggs, apparently, who also carried the virus of what the mountain people call a "valley cold" and Bart had the misfortune to catch it.

Although he awoke the next morning with a fever and a runny nose, Bart was heartened by a great Sierra storm sweeping into the area. It was a week before he was a well man and and in most of that time he watched with satisfaction as the snow piled up. On March 17 he took a busman's holiday and gauged snow along Mono Creek, his first gainful employment in months.

On March 19, Bart resumed his trek toward Yosemite. About four feet of snow made skiing easy and when he camped on the North Fork of Mono Creek that night he figured he had traveled a good twenty miles. The sky was leaden when he arose the next morning and seemed to threaten even more snow but he headed up toward Silver Pass, a climb of about 2100 feet and the eleventh of the high mountain passes on his route. On the way he went to the Silver cache, the tenth since his start, and filled his pack with supplies for a six-day journey — easily enough, he thought, to get him the thirty miles to the Devil's Postpile cache. A small storm hampered him as he crossed the pass; the white snow falling out of a white cloud made visibility almost zero as he descended the north side to camp in the upper Cascade Valley.

It was dark and stormy the next morning but he progressed well. After his brief lunch, though, the clouds lowered and again created a white-out which led Bart to serious trouble. As the storm intensified he moved hesitantly in the heavy timber of the valley floor, seeking Fish Creek as a landmark. Instead he found the stream by falling into it through the snow. He was soaked and shivering and knew he was in danger of freezing when he clambered out of the water.

A warm fire was his immediate need and he gathered fuel from the trees near the stream's bank. The fire would not start: wind whipping down the valley blew the flame away before it could take hold. He had solved this problem before and went at it again, pulling his soggy tent from the soaked pack with numbed hands and finally getting it set up. Then he kindled a fire in his frying pan inside the tent and dumped it outside into a pile of small, dry branches.

Warmth spread from it, but with the storm raging and the temperature dropping as darkness gathered, Bart decided his wet, flapping tent would not be enough protection for him in soaked clothing and sopping down quilt. Night could mean disaster unless he had a better shelter. Swinging his axe in desperation, he chopped boughs and poles to build a wickiup on the snow facing the fire; big pieces of bark peeled from the trees were worked in among the boughs as chinking.

He dragged his pack to the open front of the wickiup and in the light of the fire took out its contents. His film, camera, food and first-aid supplies had been protected by their waterproof bags, but spare clothing and the down robe he used as a sleeping bag were hopelessly soaked. By building the fire larger, Bart sought to dry the robe: it steamed in the heat but seemed to give up moisture most reluctantly. He propped it up to face the flame and turned it time and again while he fixed and ate a warm, hearty supper. Sitting in the opening of his lean-to, stoking the fire and tending his clothing for several hours, he managed to get most of his garments dry but the down robe refused to loft, its filling still wet and compressed.

The storm slackened around midnight and Bart crawled into the wickiup with the damp robe and a small canvas tarpaulin. He was asleep almost instantly, still warmed by the fire, but as the flames died for want of fuel the 12° cold crept over him. At the first glimmer of dawn he was up to rekindle the blaze and get breakfast. It must have been the worst night Bart had ever known.

He headed down the valley as soon as he had reassembled his pack, and despite difficult, slow snow underfoot he reached Crater Creek in early afternoon. There was less than a foot of coverage in the open here and he found a bare spot in a clump of trees for his camp. Before a crackling fire he spread his down quilt again and by bedtime had it dry except for some damp corners.

The temperature was two degrees above zero when he crawled out of bed the next morning, but with his clothing dry, a good night's sleep behind him and a fire soon lit, he was able to ignore the biting cold. He took pleasure in his breakfast, as he did in all his meals, absorbing the calories that would keep him going and lighten his pack as well. He moved out that morning of March 24 on new snow which had sifted down during the night.

10. Devil's Dilemma

It was March 24 — spring had arrived, at least by calendar reckoning. The sky was cloudy, a light snow was falling and the air was cold. Another storm might be on the way, Bart thought, and so he moved quickly along, headed for the little cabin at Devil's Postpile, the location of his final cache of food.

Though the route was only six miles and well known to him, he had an uneasy feeling of misgiving as he pushed ahead, noting the emptiness of the scene — even the birds had flown. Travel was difficult in the morning, but by noon the snow depth and texture had improved and his progress was better. Near the base of the symmetrical rock-and-cinder formations called the Red Cones he stopped for a hearty lunch and waxed his skis.

He had good traveling until he skied into the eerie fog of the lowering clouds and another white-out. He was not lost, for this was familiar country, but the lack of vision served to accentuate his uneasiness while he toiled toward the cabin along the Middle Fork of the San Joaquin, at the end of the basaltic piles credited to Satan. It was midafternoon when he sighted the cabin and saw smoke spewing from its crude chimney. Dogs began barking as he moved closer; two bewhiskered men came to the door and gawked at him. Neither Bart nor the interlopers could believe their eyes, for the nearest settlement was more than twenty mountain-trail miles away.

In early March, Bart's travels were nearly halted by insufficient snow. The north side of higher peaks were covered with it, but below 9,000 feet the ground was bare. Near Piute Creek he detoured from the planned route and hiked through Blayney Meadows, shown here.

Introductions were brief: the men said they were Tom and Ivanhoe. When they learned Bart's identity a feeling of tension came over them; sensing it, Bart inquired about his food cache. It was gone, used up, they said. The two men had come to the cabin at the onset of winter to start a marten farm, and though it was not clear why they had run short of food, they had robbed the cache to fill their own stomachs and those of their several dogs. Bart had put a note of explanation in each can so that, if it were found, the finder would not endanger Bart's life by making away with the food. Embarrassed, the men explained they had for some reason presumed that Bart had not made the trip and thus would not need the food.

Bart was sorely provoked. It was fifty miles to his goal in Yosemite Valley, and he had only enough food in his pack to last him two days if carefully rationed. Now after so great an effort final success seemed beyond his reach. However, Tom and Ivanhoe proposed to share what food they had, sufficient for a couple of days, and promised they would hike out to the trailhead at Mammoth Lakes and bring back provisions to keep themselves and supply Bart for the rest of what they apparently considered a dubious and somewhat pointless journey.

The inside of the cabin was a mess, housing as it did both dogs and untidy men. At any rate, Bart thought, it would be better than the little tent, and he rolled out his tarp and quilt to bed down for the night. As he did so two malemute dog teams and their drivers pulled up outside the cabin, intending to spend the night there before pushing on to the Minaret mine, a tungsten property some six miles to the west. Fortunately they had ample supplies to feed everyone supper and breakfast; when they learned of the situation they unpacked more food from the sleds and contributed it to the cause. Bart, impressed by the stout and disciplined dogs the men were driving, skied out with them the next morning to take several

A pair of Tex Cushion's dog teams get harnessed up and then head out for Mammoth Lakes to pick up supplies.

pictures of the outfit on the trail. He noted the teams were owned by Tex Cushion of Mammoth Lakes and were hired to haul supplies to the mine.

Not until March 28 did Tom and Ivanhoe decide that snow and weather conditions were right for their journey to get additional supplies. That day they snowshoed out with the dog teams returning from the mine, and other miners, who said they had enough of the mountain fastness in winter, accompanied them. The would-be marten farmers returned the following day with a disappointingly meager supply of food. They apologized, explaining that the little general store at Mammoth carried only a small stock during the winter when demand was slight.

They offered what they had, however, and Bart decided to strike out the next morning with what he knew would be lean rations. He had those fifty miles of skiing ahead, over one major pass and two secondary summits. If the weather held fair, he could reach his destination, but if a storm pinned him down, well, he would just have to stretch out the three days of food he was carrying.

It was about 7 a.m. on March 30 when Bart set out again, heading up along the frozen riverbed. He was well rested from the enforced stay at the cabin and moved rapidly shoving his skis toward his goal, glad to be alone and rid of the frustration and delay. His only concern was with the threatening weather, for a major storm now could mean disaster.

By noon he was above Agnew Meadow, six or seven miles from the cabin, and stopped for lunch. His diary does not mention the menu but no doubt Bart's thought went back to unused food in the other caches, particularly in the Humphreys cache which he had not touched because of his detour to Camp 62. Nevertheless, he knew the success of this last leg of the long journey rested on his food supply and on the weather. After

Banner Peak, in the Minarets, meant that Bart was close to the end of his great trip up the crest of the High Sierra.

A storm shrouding the peaks accompanies Bart's approach to the Devil's Postpile. Later, when he would be traveling on short rations, a delay by such weather could mean an empty stomach.

passing Agnew Meadow, Bart decided he was beyond the point of no return; Minaret Summit, four or five miles up the east wall of the canyon, could have provided an emergency escape but once beyond that turnoff he was committed to Yosemite.

In midafternoon the wind slackened and the storm clouds disappeared. Bart poled and shuffled along, climbing gradually. He found that the streams lacing the canyon were open, flowing, and he had some trouble crossing the larger ones. Despite this, his spirits soared as the weather improved and he made good time, camping that night a mile south of Agnew Pass at an elevation of 9500 feet. The campsite was new but it had the familiar wall-to-wall snow.

Bart was cold that night, and though his thermometer was down only to 14°, he arose in darkness to kindle a fire and absorb some of its warmth while he prepared an early — even for him — breakfast. He was always an early riser, claiming the habit "gave him more time to exercise an active ego."

A million morning stars were winking overhead, ready to retreat as dawn lightened the sky and the earth beneath. And so Bart watched as nature wrought her daily miracle of light on the mountain scene: the white snow on the ancient Minaret Range was the canvas, primed with the blue-gray ambiance of early dawn. Even then the dominant form of the composition was emerging as the great summits of Mt. Ritter and Banner Peak with their broken line of spires and ridges began to show in outline. From the pallet of alpenglow then, the sun brushed these upper peaks with a perfecting pink. The rosy colors spread downward while the topmost peaks caught the first golden rays of direct light. As the sun climbed in the eastern sky every rock and rampart of the range was touched with the magic of vibrant, changing color bringing life and warmth where none could be discerned before. Only the depth of the canyon was left untouched, its cold blue shadows complementing the gold above.

The scene became the essence of beauty, a picture of infinite perfection that somehow spoke to the lonely observer in strange and unusual ways. To him the marvel passed too soon, but he thought he had noted every color of the spectrum, except green, in the play of the advancing light. The green, of course, was supplied by the forests of lodgepole pine which framed the creation.

Bart had watched enthralled until the whiteness and brightness of full day aroused him to reality. Then he quickly broke camp, loaded his pack, mounted his skis and angled off toward the distant outlet of Thousand Island Lake.

He moved along rhythmically, in cadence with himself and with nature. Sliding his skis, poling his course, climbing, descending — each new cycle brought him closer to his goal. It was a vigorous but simple process that gave his active mind wide range: he thought of home, recalled earlier trips, mulled over scientific questions and looked forward to tomorrow.

A little before noon he reached the vast, frozen expanse of Thousand Island Lake and again the view demanded photographing. He hurried from vantage point to vantage point, boiling inwardly because his scanty rations denied him more time. Originally he had planned several days here in the shadow of the Minarets; once he had even considered climbing Mt. Ritter, the highest of that picturesque range.

Putting the camera away, he prepared lunch, ate swiftly and moved out, picking his own trail toward the saddle of Island Pass on the north side of the basin. But the scenes the route unfolded required his attention and it was after many stops that he found darkness coming on as he reached Rush Creek, only a few miles farther along his way. He camped beside the flowing, snow-lined stream for another short night

Beside snow-covered Thousand Island Lake, Bartholomew prepares a quick lunch. Banner Peak provides a spectacular background for the meal.

and by sunrise the next day was heading toward the top of Donohue Pass, the boundary of Yosemite National Park.

At the saddle he found nearly three feet of hard, wind-packed snow and paused only for a glance along the bright range before pushing off to begin the descent. If crossing this last barrier gave Bart satisfaction, perhaps mingled with sorrow that his trip was so near its end, it is not recorded in his diary. He does report more rapid progress as the snow and slopes aided him and he swished past the foot of Lyell Glacier and into the forest of lodgepole pine. The floor of Lyell Canyon was carpeted with smooth, firm snow and he sped along, hastening ahead of what appeared to be the threat of another mountain storm.

In the late afternoon he prepared his camp along Rafferty Creek, a tributary of the glacier-fed Lyell Creek. The broad valley ahead beckoned him on, but Bart resisted: he had covered 15 miles, he figured, the most of any day on his entire trip and probably as much as any summer traveler would do. As he set up his tent and built a fire, the upcanyon winds harried the clouds out of the sky. Relieved that he would not have to battle another storm, Bart prepared a hearty meal, breaking the pattern of light rations that he had enforced since the food problem arose at Devil's Postpile. It was just the end of another day in his winter odyssey.

By the next morning, April 2, he had reached the empty ranger's cabin at Tuolumne Meadows. Along the way he saw more and more animal tracks proving that although winter ruled the scene, spring had made its presence known. Already he could see the swelling river breaking out from beneath the white mantle. But he hurried on and, coming upon the snow-hidden road, skied with great progress. At one point he thought he might possibly reach the great valley by nightfall. While he had no schedule to meet, earlier he had set the first of April as the target date for the conclusion of the journey, but his plans were delayed by two incidents.

Near lunchtime he came across the trail of a bear so large that he removed his pack and examined the huge footprint, one of the largest he had seen. Though grizzly bears were nearly extinct in California, he thought for a moment that this mark might possibly belong to one. Bart dreaded the prospect of bumping into any bear, but he carefully examined the trail before deciding that the claw marks were too short for a grizzly.

Later on, as he came to Tenaya Lake, his plans for reaching the valley were dashed. Instead of an easy pathway across the frozen lake, he found the ice covered with three feet of water. As a result he was forced to detour along the north shoreline, where he made his last campsite. On the following morning he discovered the outlet jammed with broken ice and debris which forced the melting snow water back over the frozen surface of the lake.

11. Exit

Here is Bartholomew's final entry in his diary of the Mt. Whitney to Yosemite Midwinter Expedition, 1928-29:

> April 3: Came down Tenaya Canyon Trail to [Yosemite] Valley. Left pack at Mirror Lake and started to hunt ranger. A bootlegger picked me up and took me there. . . . tried to make a sale.

The mountains had been merciful. Bart was again within the embrace of what has been called civilization — his odyssey at an end as he declined the proffered moonshine but accepted a ride in the automobile.

The successful conclusion of the amazing mountain journey produced no signficant headlines and little publicity. By summer his accomplishment had been forgotten. Perhaps no one quite realized that he had undertaken and completed what was undoubtedly the most adventurous and strenuous piece of American mountaineering. Yet, even in this modern day of radio communication, helicopter and airplane searches and rescues, it stands as an awesome achievement.

Consider: He had spent 14 weeks in the mountains in the dead of winter, including 42 nights at elevations above 10,000 feet in temperatures which dropped as low as 14° below zero. He had traveled more than 300 miles, mostly on skis, through the roughest and highest part of California. He had climbed more than 70,000 vertical feet and, of course, descended about the same distance, crossing 13 high passes and reaching the top of two 14,000-foot peaks. He had taken nearly 400 photographs of the Sierra winter and recorded in his diary scores of observations on the bird and animal life, the snow conditions, the sounds of avalanches and many other facts as he found them, and had compiled a daily record of maximum and minimum temperatures. In preparation and accomplishment he had spent about two years of his life.

We may never know whether Bartholomew groused about the scant recognition his trip brought, for he appeared to regard it as but the beginning of a new life dedicated to the mountains. In 1932 he joined the United States Forest Service and was appointed a fire guard and ranger at Huntington Lake. Here he was at the high doorstep of some of the meadows, peaks and passes to which he was so attached. For the next twenty years he was an exemplary public servant, devoted to the mountains, to their protection and to the understanding of them, for which many people sought him out. Bart became a recognized authority on the natural history of the Sierra Nevada and was far ahead of his time in advocating strongly the enactment of antipollution regulations for the protection of forest lands.

Also in 1932, Bart discovered the other love of his life in the person of Roberta Botts of Fresno. She married and followed the rugged mountaineer to the ranger's cabin below Kaiser Ridge, where in 1935 and 1941 two sons, Phillip and Mitchell, were born.

After World War II Bart's knowledge of the Sierra fauna and flora became more widely known and he was selected to instruct special college classes in mountain study. Although he had neither degree nor title, he was sought by scholars and other experts who appreciated his expertise in mountain lore.

As a stream gauger, the rugged mountaineer traverses a steep canyon while exploring the San Joaquin watershed. Mt. Ritter rises in the distance. From such expeditions, as well as his winter-long odyssey, Bart developed a love for the Sierra that determined the course of his life.

Some called him "Mr. Sierra," a title he shared with his friend and fellow mountaineer, the late Norman Clyde.

Regardless, he never relaxed his vigilance in protecting his beloved mountains and that very devotion may have brought about his death. In 1949 he was the first man to reach the disastrous Source Point forest fire. Reacting almost by instinct, he threw himself into the battle; after thirty hours of smoke and fire he was overcome by exhaustion and smoke inhalation. He never completely recovered, and his health declined rapidly. In 1952 he was released from the Forest Service — without disability or health compensation — for advanced emphysema. He died in 1957.

His elder son, Phil, presently resides in the mountain community of Oakhurst, in eastern Madera County, where he is a biologist for the California Department of Fish and Game and a specialist in the rare and endangered golden trout. "I can remember that when my father wasn't away fighting forest fires we used to sit on the porch of our cabin at Huntington Lake and identify trees," Phil recalls. "By the time I was 12, I could name both the Latin and common name of all the trees."

While Mitchell migrated to the San Francisco Bay Area and became a successful computer system manager, he still dreams of the high country. Bart's widow has since remarried.

Bartholomew is buried in the simplest of graves in the little foothill cemetery at Tollhouse. His spirit, dedication and courage are an outstanding example of man's ennobling will to do the impossible.

Bart's Diary

Literal excerpts from the diary of Orland Bartholomew, winter 1928-29.

Dec. 31, 1928. To Rock Creek, ½ mile below timber line. Elev., 10,800. Min. temp. on Siberian Outpost: 12°. Temp at Langley Cache, midforenoon: 28°. Ave. Depth snow (all day): 2 ft. Clear, Calm. Langley Cache OK. Saw 3 Sierra Hare. Tracks indicate there are many, many fresh marten tracks. Chickadees, Douglas Squirrel.

Jan. 9, 1929. Moved up Whitney Creek to timber line at elevation of 11,000 ft. Wind rose early and is worst I have ever seen. It upset me twice on my way up the creek. It takes great chunks of the crusted snow and hurls them thru the air for hundred of feet. The loose snow it takes straight to the sky in great cork screws. . . .

Feb. 15, 1929, Min. Temp. 18°. Clear Calm. Ave. depth snow in basin 2.5 miles SE Pinchot Pass: 4 ft. . . . Practically no snow on cliffs of Woods Creek Canyon, but very deep in the bottom. Stream open only few places.

Got a fair start, but just out of camp saw the wolverine and watched him for quite a while. He was too far away to photograph and I couldn't get across the canyon without a great deal of trouble and noise.

March 2, 1929. Min. temp. 17°. Cloudy at dawn. Good NW wind. Hazy all day. Lay abed until well after day-break, had breakfast and got a supply of food from cache. Started down the hill, but found the slopes so icy that I made very poor time. Finally got down to 10,000 ft., where I found the bottom out of the snow, so that I often caved in 2 or 3 feet and was in danger of breaking my skis in the rocks. Was glad to reach the camp occupied on Feb. 21, and will wait until morning when the snow is solid before going farther. Saw Sierra Hare and marten tracks and heard conies. Also saw nutcrackers and chickadees. Saw a spider crawling over the rocks at 10,500 and a frog croaks merrily among the boulders near camp this evening.

April 1, 1929. Min temp. 14°. Ave. depth snow Donohue Pass 2.5 ft., Lyell Fk. Tuolumne at 9,500 ft., 3 ft. . . . . . Ditto at mouth Rafferty Creek. Cloudy all day. Birds — Nutcrackers, Chicadees. Animals — Coyotes, Porcupines. Snow too frozen to record small animals. Away at 8 and over Donohue. Lunched at upper end of meadows in Lyell Fork of Tuolumne and then dropped down to the mouth of Rafferty Creek. Travelling excellent on account of cloudy weather.

People of all ages gather at the summit of Mt. Whitney to view a Sierra panorama that Orland Bartholomew was the first to experience in a winter setting.

Orland Bartholomew, 1899-1957, ranks as America's most adventurous mountaineer after spending an entire winter skiing the high crest of California, alone and unaided. No other mountaineering feat has ever equaled his ambitious journey, during which he recorded the Sierra winter.

Index

• 158 •

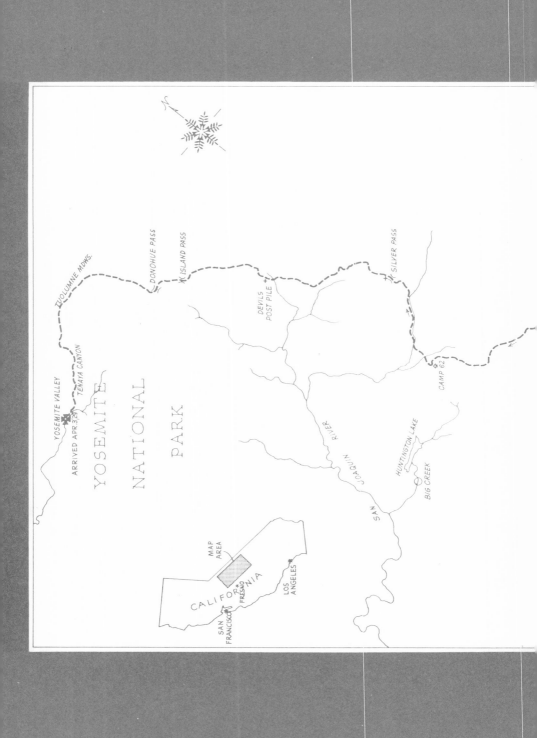